SWAT Defense
11 Man

Author: Gino Arcaro
Website: www.ginoarcaro.com
email: gino@ginoarcaro.com

All rights reserved
Copyright © Jordan Publications Inc. 2012

Jordan Publications Inc.
Canada

Editor: Matthew Dawson
Design: Jessica Ingram
Design: Shelley Palomba
Design Consultant: Luciana Millone
Logistics Manager: Jordan Mammoliti
Technical Support: Leeann King

Arcaro, Gino, 1957
ISBN 978-0-9916855-0-9
http://www.ginoarcaro.com
Printed in Canada

Gino Arcaro's Story

I started lifting as a dysfunctional 12-year-old, trying to overcome my obesity. Lifting transformed my life physically and mentally. I have been lifting for over 43 consecutive years, 100% natural. I lift almost every day. It's part of who I am and it will always be, but it doesn't define me.

At 18, I started my policing career. A few years later, I became a SWAT team officer and then at the age of 26, a detective. At the same age, I accepted the head coach position at a high school, a decision that began a lengthy volunteer coaching career. I wrote my SWAT No-Huddle Offense and Defense manuals, (and recently published them) explaining the systems I had created and refined throughout 40 seasons of coaching football at the high school, college and semi-pro levels.

After 15 years, I left policing to teach law enforcement at the local college. During the next 20 years, I became a bestselling academic author, writing 6 law enforcement textbooks that are used in colleges throughout Ontario. Also during that time, I earned a Master degree, an undergraduate degree, and Level 3 NCCP Coaching certification. Then, in 2001, I opened a 24-hour gym called X Fitness Welland Inc. The gym continues to enjoy success in its second decade of operations. eXplode: The X Fitness Training System is a book I wrote that explains my workout system, based on 40+ years of lifting.

In 2010, I left teaching to make the literary transition to motivational writer. My first book, Soul of a Lifter was published in 2011. Since then, I've added several books. Blunt Talk is the name of a series I'm writing dealing with everything from fat loss to interrogation. Soul of an Entrepreneur is another series written to enlighten business owners – current and potential. In the series, 4th and Hell, I tell "David vs Goliath" tales about my Canadian club football team playing in the United States. When my first granddaughter was born, I wrote, Beauty of a Dream and the following year, I wrote Mondo piu Bello to commemorate the birth of her cousin.

I am motivated in my writing by my belief that we all have a potential soul of a lifter. We are called to lift for life. We can lift ourselves. We can lift others.

Keep lifting,

Gino Arcaro

SWAT Spread Defense
101 Defensive Stretch Play

Twenty-first century offenses present the greatest challenge for defensive coordinators in the history of football. The post-modern era of football – spread offenses, power offenses, warp-speed, slow-speed, and everything in between. Deep Force explains our solution – The SWAT defense – a Spread defense centered on a defensive Stretch Play … a limitless system without a conventional playbook, taught by a one-man coaching staff, on both sides of the border, with open-admission student-athletes. And it's connected to our SWAT no-huddle offense, another limitless system without a conventional playbook.

Forward…and Backward

> 9-1-1…shots fired.
>
> 10-78…officer needs backup asap
>
> 921…break and enter in progress
>
> 922…violent domestic. 10-52(ambulance) en route
>
> 4th and 2 pales in comparison. So does going for 2. So does deciding to onside kick to open the game. My strongest football influence had nothing to do with football. It happened in policing. My 15-year football career taught me how to design the SWAT System – language, communications, decision-making…how to make the call.
>
> Frontline policing is a survivor's test - warp-speed life and death decision-making…making calls that deeply affect the direction of lives including your own, with no time to huddle, meet – real-life clock management. Risk, uncertainty, disappointment, failures and…critics – learning to shed all the blockers of full potential. Policing thickens skin. And lifts the Reality IQ – tacit thinking…seeing the whole board and making calls in the blink of an eye.
>
> Decision-making models are the secret to adapting to any high-pressure situation.
>
> Phonetic and digital police language is the key to warp-speed limitless communication.

Here's what this book is about and what it's not about.

What kind of defense do you run?

Unlimited. Depends on the situation – our players, our opponent, where the ball is, what's the score, what's the down and distance…everything. The teaching sequence starts with an inverted 4-2-5 that can be converted to any formation with a simple decision and simple call on the field. Our defense is defined by limitless adaptation, not by formation.

Do you have a copy of your playbook?

Don't have one.

Can you send it to me?

I meant…we don't have a playbook. No Diagrams, nothing to memorize.

Deep Force is different than any football book you will ever read. It's about the most unique defense in football – the SWAT Defense, an unlimited defense with NO conventional playbook, that's connected to the SWAT offense. A playbook replaced by a dictionary. Limitless, paperless, seamless…linked to a no-huddle spread offense to form one system that lets an unconventional team survive. A SPREAD DEFENSE based on a defensive STRETCH Play. And, it's about doing what seems impossible – one-man staff coaching a Canadian collegiate club team in the United States, on the road for every game, with open-admission players. The SWAT system has been a way to close Goliath-sized competitive gaps since 1985, at 3 levels (high school, post-secondary, semi-pro), with the most limited resources imaginable – human, financial, physical.

∞

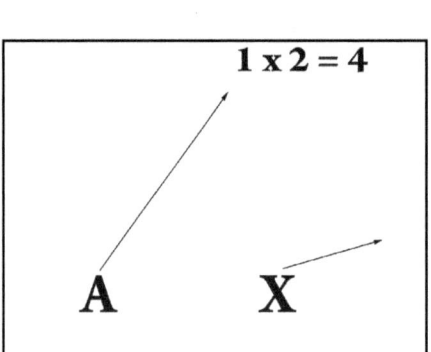

This Diagram is an example of what this book is about – the connection of SWAT Defense and SWAT Offense. What you see is a partial concept that applies to both SWAT Defense and SWAT Offense – a partial blitz concept and a partial passing concept using exactly the same player code-names and sprint tracks.

A (Alpha) is the conventional defensive end.

X (X-Ray) is the X-Man, the MVP – Most Versatile Player…a multi-purpose player who can play at 4 different levels – level 1-4. Conventionally called strong safety, the X-Man is a player without a conventional position. He has to be able to play defensive line, linebacker, strong safety, and free safety.

The same two code-names are used in the SWAT spread no-huddle offense. Alpha designates a wide receiver. X-Ray designates an inside receiver, the 4th receiver who shifts out of the backfield from the conventional fullback position. The offensive X-Man has to be able to play every offensive skill position – online receiver, offline, wide, slot, inside, tight, blocker, feature ball-carrier…even QB.

When you drop the labels, the defensive end becomes another MVP – a key to the SWAT system…drop the labels and open the potential.

The above Diagram shows both a defensive and offensive concept.

Alpha sprints a 75-degree track.

X-Ray sprints a 30-degree track.

Same job, different angle. Both jobs can be learned simply by changing the first step.

Together, the two tracks form a joint defensive and offensive partial concept:
i. Defensively, it represents a partial blitz concept that binds from the frontside or backside;
ii. Offensively, it represents a partial pass concept that binds any coverage from the frontside or backside.

In our reality of one-man coaching staff and 2-way players, this concept has dual-purpose. One lesson, 2 players… 4 jobs learned.

∞

Deep Force is a coaching survival manual – how to beat the odds, how to beat extreme adversity…and make an impact. The SWAT Defense is a radically different defensive system and even more radically different philosophy designed by a coach who thinks farther outside the box than any football coach – in two countries.

Deep Force is not a conventional defensive playbook. It's about a no-playbook SWAT defensive system that lets a defense make no-huddle calls and rapid-fire audibles to adapt to any formation and any situation, using the police communication system and simple decision-making models…and connects to the SWAT Spread No-Huddle Offense.

Like the SWAT Spread No-Huddle Offense, the SWAT Defense is a SPREAD defense, a system that can attack spread offenses and power offenses without changing the system. The SWAT Defensive system includes a solution to the post-modern offensive challenge – it's a Spread No-Huddle Defense.

∞

The SWAT Defensive System features:

- limitless capacity,

- NO conventional playbook,

- a two-way connection,

- warp-speed, no-defensive-huddle play-calling,

- cross-border exchange,

- forced deep passing as the base philosophy,

- spread defense capacity, and

- defensive STRETCH PLAY.

Deep Force is about believing in no limits. The SWAT defense is capable of unlimited formations, unlimited blitzes, unlimited coverages, unlimited plays…change without changing the system.

Deep Force is about thinking outside the box – literally and figuratively. What separates the SWAT Defense from other defensive systems is how it connects to the SWAT offense. Same language, same communication style, same decision-making, shared techniques….with no playbook, no limits, and no huddle.

We are not bi-lingual. We don't have two languages for offense and defense. We have one official language that applies to the entire SWAT system – offense and defense.

No conventional playbook with thousands of Diagrams to memorize. In the SWAT system, players follow a simple 5-step process that I learned in frontline policing: analyze, decide, communicate, translate, execute – at warp-speed.

Build the big picture with as much information as possible, see the whole board, recognize the problem/situation, make a call, communicate the call without a meeting/huddle, use the phonetic alphabet and 10-code/900-code system, translate what was said….put the play in motion. Don't blink. The system tells players what to do and how to communicate it. Two types of 'mental mistakes' have been eliminated – what call to make, remembering assignments. The call is recognized, not guessed.

Deep Force is about doing what it takes. Like the SWAT offense, the defensive plays are called at the LOS without a huddle, by joining partial concepts. SWAT defensive plays don't have names – they have instructions. And memorization is replaced by translated. Informed decision-making to make the call. No studying a 1,000 page playbook. No memorizing plays. No recall of Diagrams in a playbook. Regurgitation is replaced by understanding.

Deep Force is about overcoming obstacles. The SWAT Defense is a solution to lack… insufficiency and deficiency - not enough coaches, not enough players, not enough talented players, not enough practice time, and not enough money. Very few coaches want to work for free. Canadian players miss practices – that's part of the Canadian football culture. Canadian high school players don't get as many reps in general and as many meaningful reps as American high school players, preventing Canadians from developing skills at the same rate – an unbalanced exchange rate.

Deep Force is about making it happen. The SWAT system easily converts from 11-man to12-man…American or Canadian football. An equal exchange rate. SWAT has worked on both sides of the border - sometimes on consecutive weeks - to overcome overwhelming challenges: (a) one-man coaching staff. A 3-way coordinator. One coach calling all the plays – and making substitutions (b) 25-30 man roster. Every year we start with over 100 players. Every year, about 66% don't want to meet the full-time commitment. This didn't start in the social media era known as the 21st century. It dates back to 1985, my first season as a high school head coach. We've had 3 undefeated seasons with 3 different teams, none of which had a roster larger than 25. When the first-string linebacker is the second-string fullback , the third-string guard, and 4th-string tight end, an innovative system is needed. And when defensive experience is limited, you can't limit experience players to one defensive position – move him around, from level to level. Then do the same with other experienced players – move them from level 1 to level 4. Eventually, traditional positions become slang terms – points-of-references to teach new positions that you have to invent. 'Strong safety' is a job title – but, not the only job.

Deep Force is a defense mechanism – force them to go deep on the field and to go deep inside. Neither is automatic. Unless they have trained to go deep, they'll crack under the pressure. Forced deep passing is the base philosophy. Deep passing is the first teaching phase for the entire system – offense and defense. We don't teach the SWAT system in isolation – we teach both defense and offense together and connect both to the deep passing game. There are 3 phases of both the offense and defense – deep passing, running plays, short passing…in that order of rep investment. We invest 100% of reps into passing deep and defending deep passing, at the start of installation – not one rep on running plays, not one rep on short passing…until the deep game is fully installed on both sides of the ball. There are 3 reasons why deep passing is the first teaching phase for both defense and offense:

1. **Need**. One-man coaching staff and 2-way players. We have to conserve teaching time – maximize every second, capitalize on every rep. Teach deep passing on offense and teach how to stop it at the same time – 2 lessons in one.

2. **Philosophical**. We believe:

    (a) forcing deep passing by the opponent is the best way to close a huge competitive gap

    (b) run defense is built into pass defense, not vice-versa. Run defense and pass defense are not isolated – they're connected. The run is defended on the way to the quarterback. The pass rush defends the run.

    (c) forcing deep passes stops the offense from running

    (d) deep passing generally gets the least reps.

    (e) the longer the ball is in the air the greater the chance of change of possession and points – interception and defensive TD. What you focus on grows.

3. **Deep passing is the teaching point-of-reference for the SWAT language and decision-making models – on defense and offense.** The SWAT language and decision-making models can't be taught versus running plays and short passing. The system won't make sense if running or short passing is taught first. SWAT deep passing opens the border on offense and closes the border on defense. This book – book #1 – teaches the basics of system... SWAT101. Four bases – 4 base defenses that can convert to any formation, any play.

∞

Deep Force has many meanings:
- Force the offense to go deep on the field.
- Force the offense to do deep inside – going deep is not automatic. Only those willing and capable can go deep. Only those who have prepared can go deep without cracking under pressure.
- Pressure is a deep force. It's connected to going deep. Pressure invites the deep pass, stops the deep pass, makes you crack or thrive and survive.
- There's a force deep inside, if you can reach it.
- The deep force is unstoppable.
- The deep force can stop any force from going deep.
- Deep force connects with a pass rush.
- Deep force makes an impact.
- You can't go deep on demand – you can only go as deep your training.
- The deep-force connection. Going deep and force upfront are connected. One stops the other.

- Defense has to be a deep force.
- Use of deep force stops any attack.
- Use of deep force starts with a rush.
- Use of deep force ends with a rush.
- Turn on the switch to apply deep force.
- Turn on the switch to fight deep force.
- Beat deep force with deep force.
- Forcing them to go deeper than they trained for….then deeper.
- Deep down, we know that 'deep down' is not a comfortable place.
- Force as many 'deep downs' as possible.
- DEeep Force — DEFense

Force the opponent to go deeper than they are willing or capable of going. 'Deep downs' are scoring opportunities – for the defense.

∞

The 3 primary objectives of the base SWAT defense are:

i. stop the strong-side stretch,

ii. stop 3-step short passing, and

iii. invite deep passing.

The strong-side stretch play is the greatest threat to a mismatched team. We are mismatched annually. The talent imbalance is inherent to our team mission of providing a second chance to unrecruited student-athletes. If we can't stop the strong-side stretch, we'll get pounded into the ground and lose by lopsided scores.

Stopping the strong-side stretch is the first priority regardless of who we play. The base SWAT defense is an unconventional formation directly intended to side-track the strong-side stretch by closing the borders of the stretch play track.

Three-step passing is deadly against a physically mismatched team because it is an extension of the running game. Short passing has the same ground and pound effect of power running. The base SWAT is intended to pressure every receiver, especially the inside receivers, by disrupting the all-important timing needed for the short-passing success.

The combined effect of the first two objectives leads to the third objective – invite them to go deep. The deeper the better – for five reasons:
- while the ball is in the air, no one has possession of the ball,
- the longer the ball is in the air, the greater the chance for a big play – interception or QB sack,
- pressuring a QB is much easier for a mismatched team than pressuring a stronger ground and pound attack,

- if they're passing, they're not running, and
- a strong running team generally is not a strong passing team because of imbalanced rep investment. Invite them to do what they are not great at doing.

A system is connected to its philosophy. The philosophy is connected to the journey – where you've been, what you've experience, what you've learned. The SWAT Defense is a playbook system based on a teaching and training philosophy. This is why the system's philosophy is included in this book. The philosophy is an integral part of what is taught – it's is the system.

The philosophy was shaped outside football, during an unconventional coaching journey that I make available to players so they understand the reasons for my thinking – the rationale for my decision-making. The Journey that formed the rationale for the SWAT Defense is important to understand why we do what we do. The Journey is published on our website. Please visit www.ginoarcaro.com. We hope you will read it to learn how the SWAT System evolved and understand why we do what we do.

The BASICS
SWAT 101: The Stretch Play

SWAT mission statement: Attack, don't defend. It's impossible to defend without attacking. Not possible. The name "defense" itself is counter-productive and counter-intuitive – "defense" suggests defend, which can't be done. There are many myth associated with defending. One is that attacking and defending are separate strategies. They're not – they're the same. "Defense" should be renamed "attackers."

∞

Here's exactly what I teach and the order I teach it, as a one-man coaching staff to reach a limitless defense without a playbook:

- **Four bases** – four base formations but I start only with the first 2.

- **SWAT language** – a one-page dictionary that explains our terminology.

- **53 communication system** – SWAT defensive play-calling; how to apply the language and call a play.

- **Decision-making models.**

With all due respect to the thousands of players I coached in my life, the majority are not honour/honor roll students. The majority have been academic-underachievers and non-achievers. But, this teaching plan has worked. I have taught this system alone, without classroom time, and rarely with paper supplements. Almost everything I teach is on the field. Classroom time has been impossible either because of limited time or limited space or both. I rarely have given out written reading material.

Full installation takes less than 8 hours. Not 8 total, continuous hours of teaching defense– four two-hour practices… the usual week one of Canadian high school and college pre-season. Tuesday to Friday following Labour/Labor Day. One-a-days for four days. I've never had two-a-days in almost 3 decades as head coach at 3 levels of football – no time, no money, no building. This is why I had to design a system to connect defense to offense. This is the rationale for my teaching plan.

It has never failed to work. Fully installed limitless defense in 8 hours of total practice time. Limitless defense system installed before the end of week #1 of pre-season.

Four Bases

I start by introducing 4 base formations on the field, after I introduce the SWAT no-huddle offense language, communication, and decision-making models. Swat offense first, SWAT defense second. This sequence fast-tracks teaching defense by establishing the front-end of the connection.

All four bases look the same but each one has a distinct purpose. Small changes, big differences. The sum is bigger than the parts. A few small changes add up to limitless potential.

All four bases are taught against a 21 formation (2 backs – single TE to our left), using both shotgun and I-formation. The 21formation serves as a dual purpose point-of-reference - it's the base SWAT offensive formation, the first of limitless formations we use on offense, and it's the most common base offense we face.

First base: Xpress SWAT 2 Lock

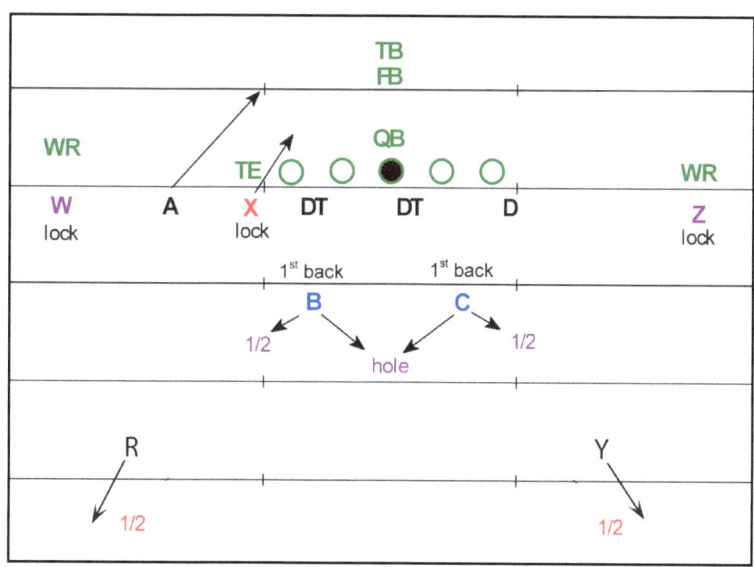

Second base : fleXpress SWAT 3

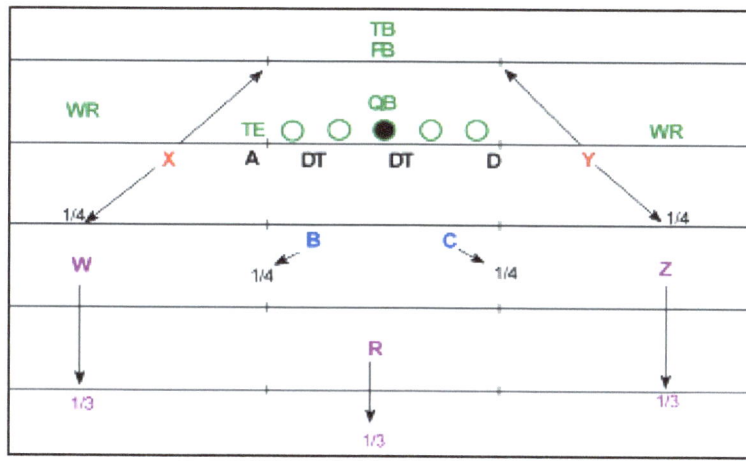

Third base: AXchange SWAT 2 Lock

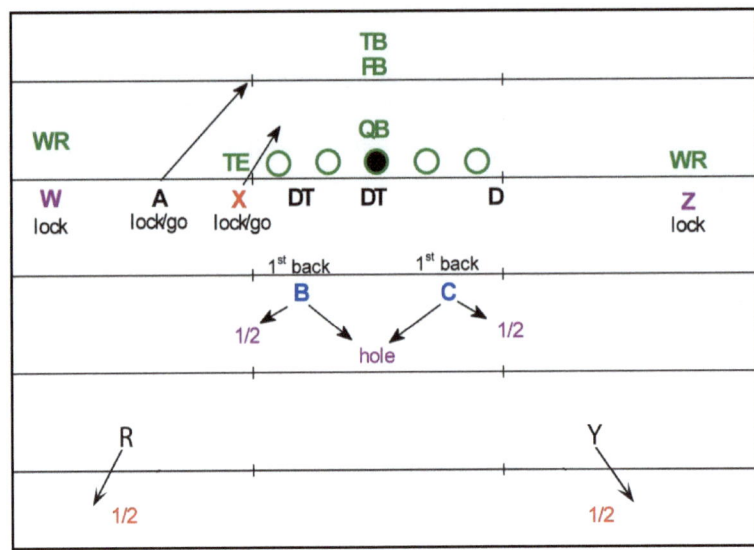

Fourth base: flAXchange SWAT 3 Lock

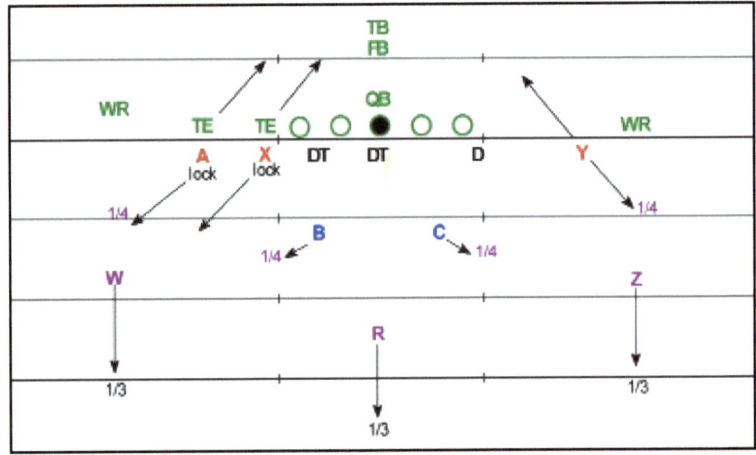

The SWAT defense doesn't have just one base defense, it has four base formations. Each one uses at least 2 strong safeties. 1st base and 2nd base include 2 strong safeties. 3rd base and 4th base include 3 strong safeties.

Ten introductory key points of the SWAT defensive system are:

1. Conventional defensive positions are limiting. Traditional names of defensive positions limit the mindsets of coaches and players. Defensive line limits plays to specific assignments. So does linebacker, defensive end, defensive tackle, and every other defensive name that has been used forever. Position name stereotype players, which ultimately restricts what a defense is capable and willing to do. We use conventional defensive names only as points-of-reference to teach rookies. Afterward, we transition to code-names.

2. In our language/system, strong safety is an MVP – most versatile player…a 4-level player capable of playing conventional levels of positions - DE, ILB, SS, FS.

3. Conventional defensive formation numbering is replaced by a Box Ratio and SWAT Language. What kind of defense do you run? I answer "4-2-5 base" only as a point-of-reference but I have never taught the phrase 4-2-5 to players and never use the phrase 4-2-5 during the season. I use 4-2-5 only to introduce the SWAT defense because it has similar elements to a 4-2-5 but it is a system that builds any formation necessary to defend the post-modern offensive attacks that includes the widest range of offensive formations and offensive formations in the history of football. The SWAT defense can convert to limitless formations – any formation from spread defense to power defense. Instead of the conventional numbering system (ie: 4-3, 3-4), we use BOX Ratios and SWAT Language to call defense. In this book, conventional numberings are included as teaching points-of-reference.

4. 2-sided Box… on both sides of the LOS. Generally, the box is defined as the area in front of the LOS from EMOL to EMOL (outside shoe of end men on-line). We re-defined box to include the are behind the LOS into the backfield, extended from the front box. Front box plus back box.

5. Box ratio is a two digit number, ie: 65, 74 – the ratio of inside-the-box and outside-the-box defenders first digit refers to the number of players inside the box, the second digit refers to the number of outside the box players. Outside the box players are called "space defenders."

6. There are 2 Box Ratios - pre-snap and post-snap box ratios. Usually, they are the same but they don't have to be. The defensive coordinator can change the ratio with post-snap box entries – space defenders entering the box after the snap, while the play is in-progress.

7. Post-snap box ratio is more important. The significance of the number of box defenders is predicting the blocking scheme – run blocking or pass protection – and deciding what play to make. Generally, the focus is on the number of pre-snap box defenders – counting the number of defenders aligned in the box. But, the real issue is the number of post-snap box defenders – how many defenders play inside the box while the play is in-progress. Pre-snap box numbers provides circumstantial evidence of how many defenders need to be blocked. But post-snap numbers is the actual evidence – the best evidence. Changing the number will disrupt blocking by preventing the right call from being made. The SWAT base defense changes the ratio from a 65 pre-snap (6 in the box - 5 in space, outside the box) to a 74 post-snap – the 65/74 defense. Starts as a 65 box ration, finishes as 74. The 65-74 replaces the 4-2-5 name.

8. One-page SWAT language Diagram. The unique SWAT language is the basis of the limitless, no-playbook system. Based on the police communication system, the entire language fits on one page.

9. Decision-making models. SWAT calls are made at the LOS without a huddle and can be converted to fit any offensive formation without an audible call. The change is automatic. But the system is not dictated by the offense. We play our own game but fit the situation when needed.

10. Change the perspective, change the outcome. Two Diagrams are needed to teach and learn defense. Generally, defensive play Diagrams are configured from the defense's perspective – from the bottom of the page upward. That Diagram explains only half the story. A second Diagram is needed to view the defense from the offense's perspective. Flip the Diagram – top of the page to the bottom. Seeing the defense from the offense's perspective deepens understanding of the defense. This same principle is used to teach the SWAT no-huddle offense in Pass Rush.

∞

One-Page Language: Position Names

Legend

Blue = Defense POSITIONS & CODE NAMES

Red = Offense, showing a 21 Shotgun formation: 2-backs & 1-TE to the defense left

Purple = Numbering of offensive eligible receivers from outside-in (1-3, both sides of center)

Black = Gap lettering (A-D, both sides of center)

Grey = Level one (defensive line) alignment numbering system (0-8, both side of center)

Orange = Blitz lanes: even to the right (2-8), odd to the left (1-7), zero to the midline

Green = Strong safety alignments (X & Y) – 4 levels, on both sides of the midline

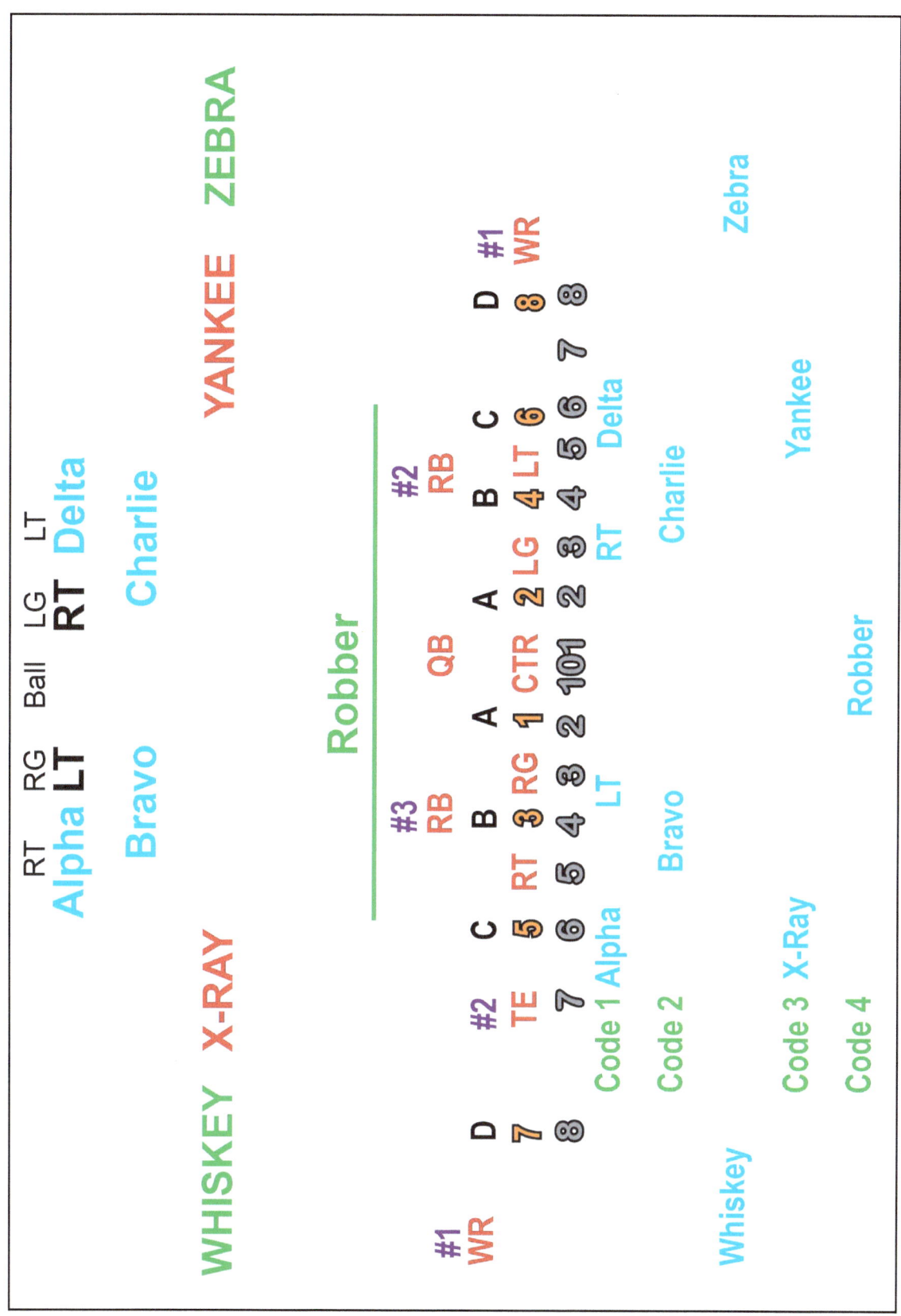

SWAT Language
The One-Page Dictionary

This is another connection that links SWAT defense to SWAT no-huddle offense – a language based on police communication that fits on one page. A one-page dictionary of terminology that can communicate limitless defensive calls – alignments and assignments…coverage and pressure.

53 Communication

53 Communication is another connection that links the SWAT defense to SWAT no-huddle offense – a communication system that replaces memorization with translation. The base call using SWAT language and 53 communication is: 41 – code 14, Bravo 1, 921.

"53 communication" is defined as a sentence that conveys the defensive call. 53 refers to the maximum/minimum elements – 5 maximum, 3 minimum. Using the range of 5 maximum elements and 3 minimum elements, the sentence communicates both alignment and assignments to all 11 defenders. One sentence with a 3-5 element range.

The 53 communication system allows limitless calls.

Examples:

- **Minimum 3-element call:**   41, ____, Code 14, _____, 921

- **4-element call:**   41, ____, Code 14, Bravo 1, 921

- **Maximum 5-element call:** 3   3, Mike, Code 12, Charlie 1, 911

Five total elements: three (1, 3 and 5) are mandatory; two (2 and 4) are optional.

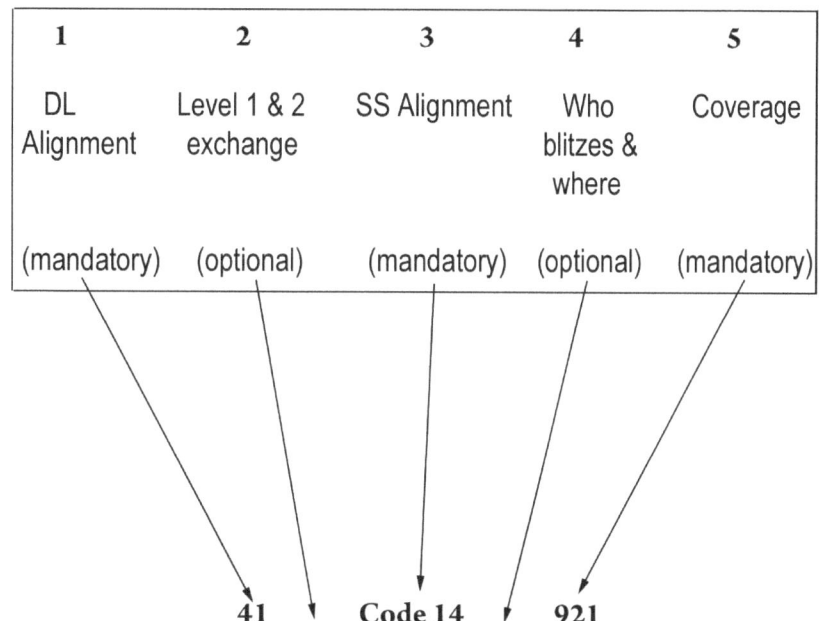

Key Points

- Element 1 instructs all level 1 defenders where to align, using a minimum of 2 digits- first digit is the left DT. Second digit is the right DT. The two defensive ends automatically align on outside shade of EMOL.

- Element 2 exchanges DLs and LBs to created limitless conversions from 4-2-5 to 3-3-5, 5-2, etc. alignments. This element instructs linebackers to re-align from level 2 to level 1 and DTs to realign from level 1 to level 2. The LB's code name is used to re-align. Example: "Bravo" means realign to nose-tackle. "Mike" tells the left DT to align at middle linebacker.

- Element 3 instructs the "strong safeties" where to align, using CODE 2-digits: digit 1 aligns X; digit 2 aligns Y. When three strong safeties are used, 3 digits are called corresponding with A,X,Y in that order.

- Element 4 communicates who is blitzing and where. Linebacker code name plus hole gap number ie: Bravo 1 – Bravo blitzes through one hole (left A gap). The left tackle rushes away, into B gap.

- Element 5 instructs coverages. All coverages are called with a 3-digit number starting with 9 which means "the coverage is". The second number (ie: 2) means the coverage "family" ie: 2 deep/Cover 2. The third digit (ie: 1) means the coverage "concept" ie: man/press. Limitless concepts can be designed and numbered from one to infinitum (ie: "2" = man/soft – 5 yards)

- Elements 1, 3, and 5 are mandatory in every call.

- Elements 2 (LB realign on level 1) and 4 (blitzes) are optional.

∞

SCORES Decision-Making Model

Defensive coordinators have the greatest challenge in the history of football because offensive coordinators found the secret – the rules allows for limitless offensive formations. From spread to power formations, offenses have few limits – a minimum of 7 players on the LOS. That's it. But defenses truly have no limits – there is no minimum LOS requirement for defenders.

SCORES is another connection to the SWAT no-huddle offense. Same terminology and same decision-making concepts used to make defensive calls. SCORES allows the defense to change from a SPREAD defense to a Power defense. Here are the rules governing the model:

>Scan
>Observe
>Recognize

Solution: Spread or Shrink. 5S model: spacing, free safeties, strong safeties, security, search.

Spacing: means box defenders defender alignment is governed by: (a) a relationship to the number of interior blockers (5,6, or 7), and (b) equal distance of separation.

Free safeties: There is a relationship between the number of level 4 defenders and receivers who align outside the backfield. Two level 4 defenders is the starting point. That number converts in relation to the number of backs and receivers.

Strong safeties: aka MVP. Each base formation has a minimum of 2. They can align at any of the 4 defensive levels.

Security: Offense has the onus to protect their QB – security management. Defense has the onus to attack QB protection and cause security mismanagement.

Search: Alignment and assignment has one objective – ball tracking. Search for the ball, find the ball, and get possession of the ball. The defense has the same overall purpose as offense – 2 Ps. Possession and points.

We make calls at the LOS, informed decisions, to either: (a) make an original call without a huddle, or (b) change the original defensive call by converting coverage in accordance to full ratio formula, a chart that matches coverage against offensive formation

Two general rules govern our decision-making – how to make a call:

Rule #1: play your own game.

Rule #2: strategize and improvise - customize calls that fit the situation and still let you play your own game.

SCORES is achieved by reading the opposing using the same Board Theory of reading the defense used in the SWAT no-huddle:

>See the whole board
>Know the situation
>Make the call
>Remember it

The Board Theory starts with formation classification – classifying the offensive formation. Offenses are divided into classifications by full ratio – a 3-digit number that quantifies total TEs, backs, and space receivers (receivers-outside-the-box - ROTB). The SWAT offensive formation chart lists 9 full ratios, representing 9 offensive formations. This classification chart has 5 columns:

1) # of backs

2) # of tights end

3) Back-Tight end ratio

4) # of space receivers (ROTB – receivers outside the box)

5) Full ratio: a 3-digit number that equal 5.

   digit 1 = # of backs

   digit 2 = # of TEs,

   digit #3 = # of space receivers (ROTB)

Backs	TEs	RB-TE ratio	ROTB	Full Ratio
2	1	2x1 (21)	2	212
2	2	2x2 (22)	1	221
2	0	2x0 (20)	3	203
1	1	1x1 (11)	3	113
1	2	1x2 (12)	2	122
1	0	1x0 (10)	3	103
Zero	1	0x1 (01)	4	014
Zero	2	0x2 (02)	3	023
Zero	0	0x0 (00)	5	005

∞

SWAT Audible System: Conversion Chart

The base call is 41 – code 14 - 921. That's the SWAT language for the first base formation called Xpress SWAT 2 Lock.

SCORES is the decision-making model that structures how to make the defensive call and how to change it. Scanning, observing, and recognizing the offensive formation leads to Solution – the last letter in SCORES.

The SWAT Audible System is a Conversion Chart that reaches the Solution, the decision to keep the call or change it, and if a change is needed, to what call exactly. The SWAT Audible System is composed of 10 simple rules that govern all audible/changes – how to convert coverage and intention to fit a specific situation while being able to play your own game:

1. Twin receivers + single TE (WRs on same side opposite from TE):

   - cornerbacks cover receivers - #1

   - cornerbacks cover twins - when #1 moves to #2 on twin side with or without motion

   a) if WRs shift/motion, cornerbacks chase. Coverage does not bump over.

   – chase above the box, not through it. Then, align nose-on and lock on the receiver. No change in assignment. Diagram 13

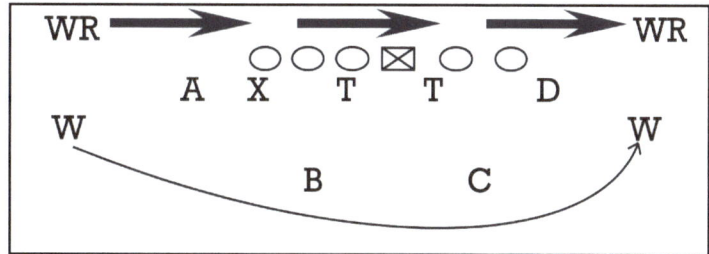

   b) same rule when receivers align on the same side from the huddle instead of motion – cornerbacks always cover receivers. Diagram 14

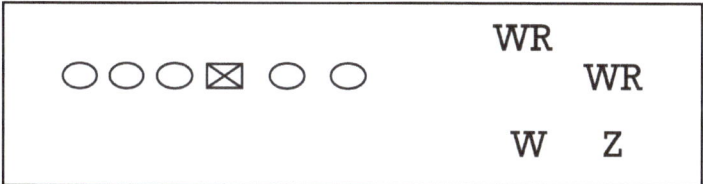

2. X covers single TE, regardless of what side TE aligns on and regardless of number of backs. The DE on the TE side flexes. Diagram 15

3. #4 receiver – with or without shift/motion: convert to cover 1 by FS covering #4. (a) If motion, FS on side of the 4th receiver drops down to cover 4th receiver without pressing - nose-on @ 5 yards. Diagram 16

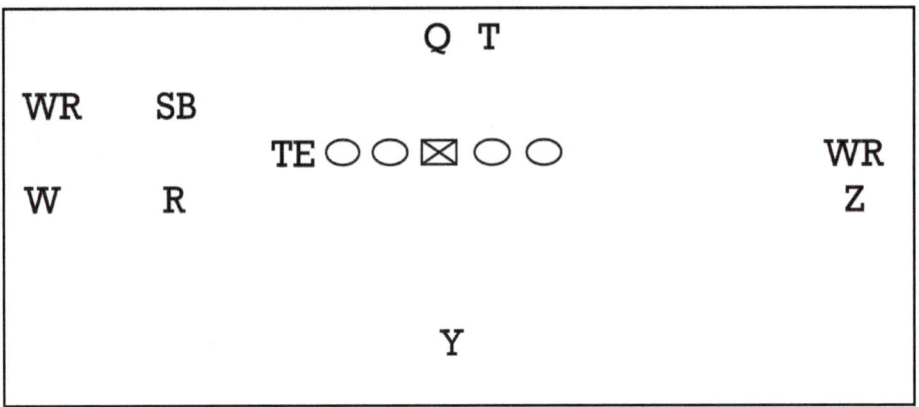

(b) If no motion, Y covers 4, R becomes the midline FS. No other assignments change. Diagram 18

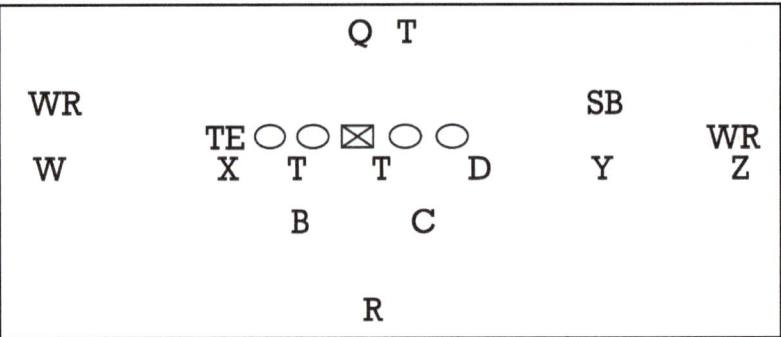

*If RB motions outside the box to WR, LBs do not chase/re-align. Diagram 17

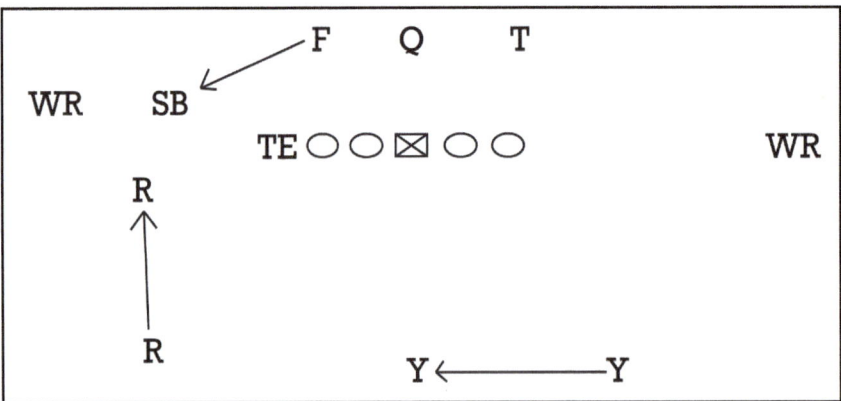

4. #5 receiver = convert to cover zero/no press and rush 6. Second FS covers #5. All DB 5 nose-on, 5 yards off. CHARLIE BLITZES to generate max pressure – 6-on-5.

5. Double TE = SS + CB exchange. Both SSs press + lock (X on defensive left, Y on def. right), cornerback replaces Y on level 4 + double-flex DE except when the DT aligns at NT. Never leave 2 uncovered OL side-by-side. Diagram 19

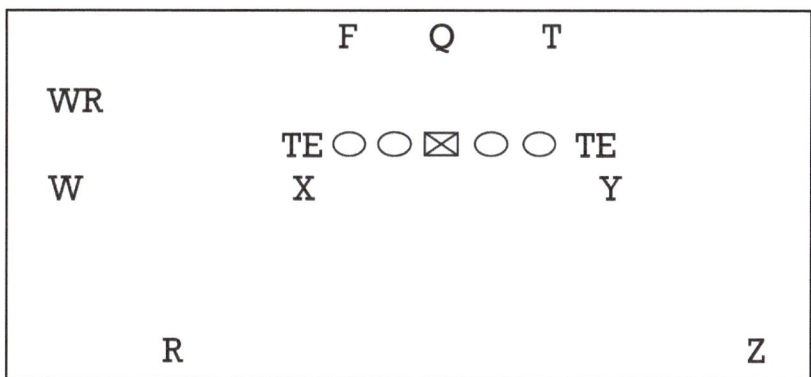

6. If zero TE = X covers #2 as a level 3 SS + no DE flex – DE on OT's outside shoulder.

   A) If 2 backs, X covers #2. Diagram 20

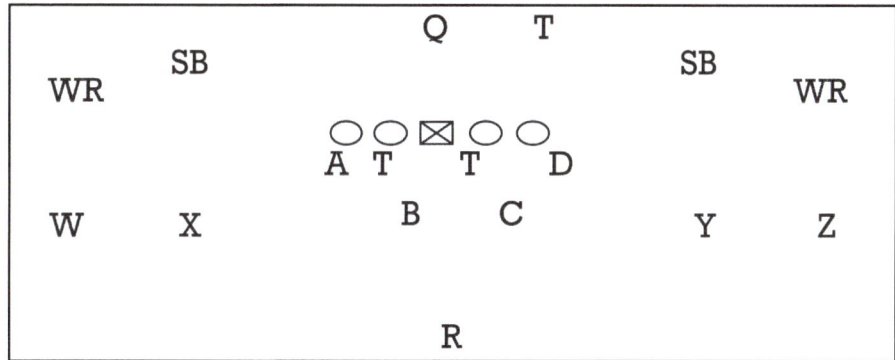

   B) If 1 or zero backs, X covers #2 on defensive left. Diagram 21

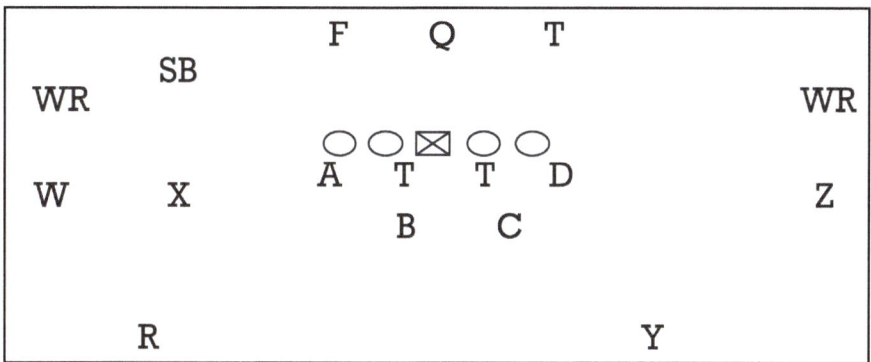

Diagram 22

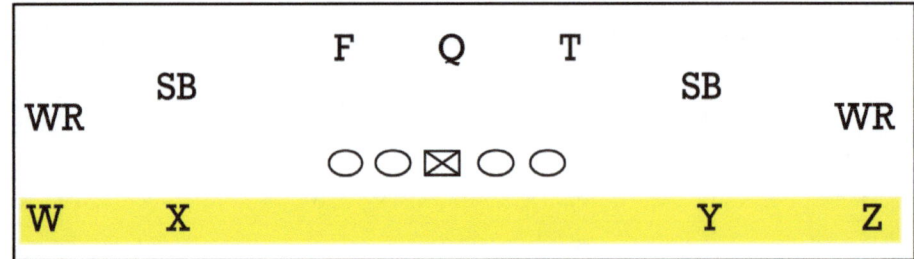

7. DT exchange: (a) 41 to strongside in single TE (b) 33 if no single TE; if doubleTE, or zero-TE, both DTs realign to nose-on-guard (33) and both DTs are assigned double A-gap with 30-degree rush (first step to A-gap midpoint and uppercut). Double A –gap pressure is an essential basic for maximum pressure. 6 run defenders aim at 3 pressure points. In double-TE, Bravo and Charlie still align in B gap but Bravo exchanges blitz lane from A to B, to maintain BAA blitz;, Charlie has dual-responsibility (B to RB/hole).   **Diagram 24**

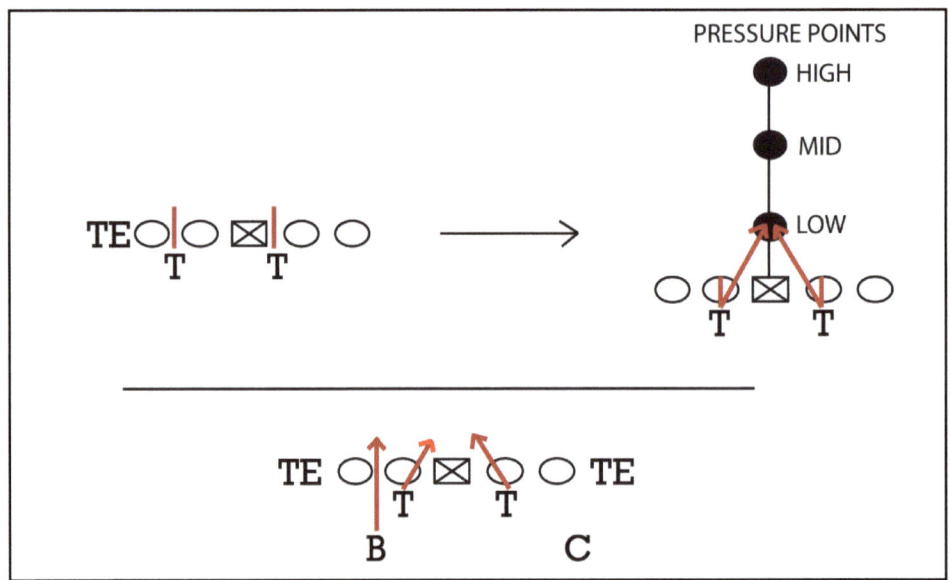

8. If single-TE aligns left, the call reverses sides - exchanges: DT exchange alignments; they align 41 to TE; Bravo and Charlie exchange assignment; Alpha and Delta exchange flexing. **Diagram 25**

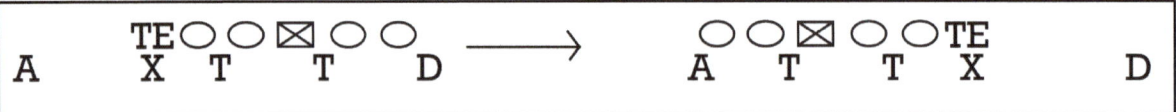

9. If RB releases, Charlie covers him man-to-man. If RB blocks, Charlie drops to hole. Diagram 26

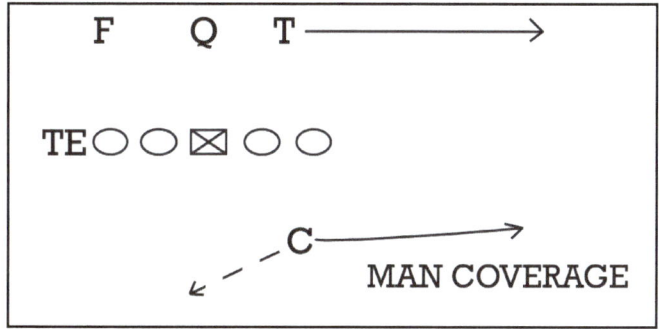

10. If single-back shotgun aligns on Bravo's side, Bravo and Charlie exchange assignment – the ILB opposite to the single shotgun back blitzes strongside A gap. Diagram 27

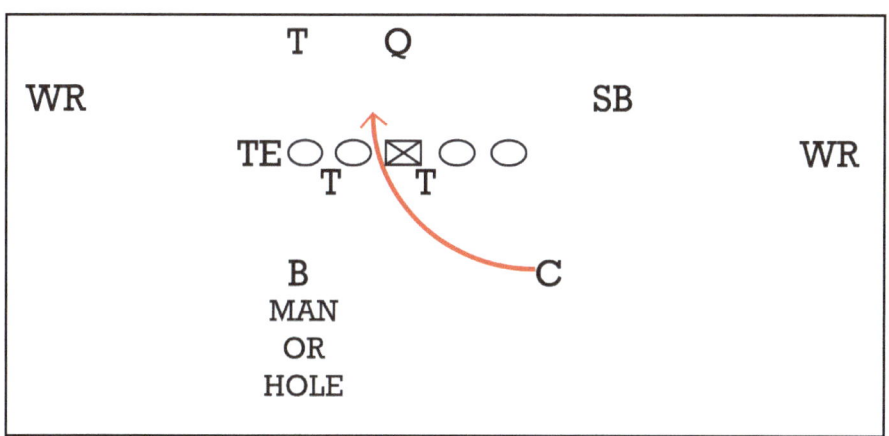

Summary:

- 2 backs: corners cover #1, X TE/#2

- 1 back + 1 TE: W and Z = #1 or twins; X = TE, y=#4

- 1 back + 0 TE: same except X = #2 left side

- zero backs = combine all 10 rules

∞

First Base: Spread Defense

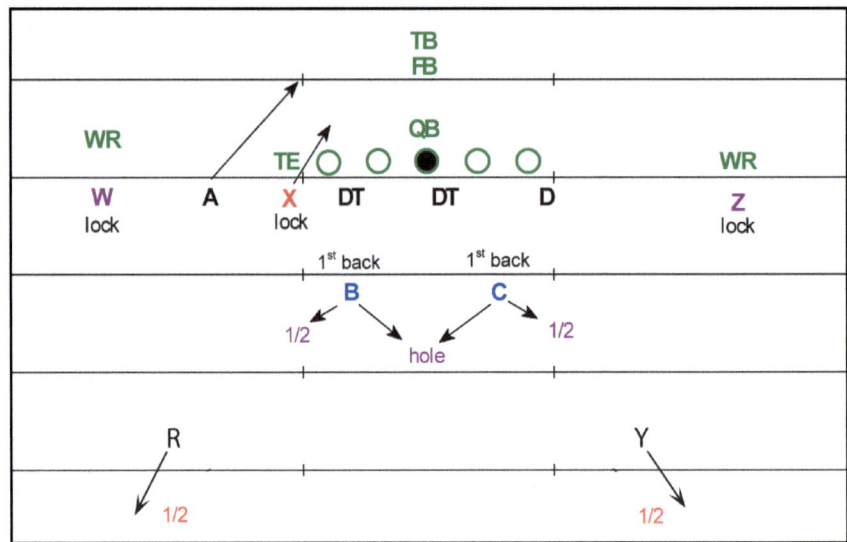

The next step in the installation plan is teaching the key elements of First Base:

- 1st base resembles a 4-2-5 man with an unconventional alignment. 4-2-5 is only a point-of-reference to explain first base to those accustomed to naming defenses with a 3-digit number. But, first base is not a true 4-2-5…or a true 4-3, or a true 3-4. Instead, we call it Xpress SWAT 2 Lock or 65-74 (box ratio).

- 1st base is a SPREAD defense, a strongside spread – spread to the single TE side.

- Xpress means X (X-Man) presses the TE on the LOS. For point-of-reference, the X-Man resembles the traditional strong safety position but he's more than that. In first base, the X-Man aligns on level one like a DE, directly nose on the TE. His two assignments in SWAT 2 lock are: (i) man coverage on the TE. The X-Man has to learn to play Bravo on the SWAT offense, the Big End traditionally called the tight end. The X-Man bench pressures the TE on every play – bench pressures is our language for a bench press bump and run technique. Bench pressure is the X-Man's tactic to complete his mission - battle the TE and wear down the TE physically and mentally. Break his will. Versus the run, the X-Man's job is to run the inside border of the strong-side stretch play. The X-Man plays TE in reverse. He also plays the RB stretch play in reverse.

- SWAT 2 Lock means 2-deep man cover with nose-on pressure on every receiver who aligns outside the backfield, whether they are online or offline. 2-deep, lock, and load on every wide and inside receiver. The 2 deep safeties are run defenders first, pass defenders second.

- First base has a 65-74 box ratio. The offense sees a pre-snap 65 box ratio. But, versus the run, the post-snap ration changes to 74 because A (Alpha – the conventional DE) rushes from outside the box and enters the behind-the-LOS box after the snap, while the play is in progress. Alpha sprints the outside border of the strong-side stretch – he plays the RB stretch play in reverse. The box ratio changes to 83 when the frontside safety enters the box after the snap.

- The purpose of the Xpress is to:
  i. Take away the strong-side stretch play by occupying both borders and filling the alley with ILBs and deep safeties. Every stretch play has an initial track – aim point at the TE's heel and two borders, outside and inside the TE, and the entrance to the track built by the 2 borders. The stretch play is a discretionary off-tackle play, where the ball-carrier has a choice… a decision to make about what track to take – stay on the initial track or change lanes inside or outside. The keys to stopping the strong-side stretch are: (a) remove the ball-carrier's discretion – force him to stay on the initial track. Then squeeze the track by closing the borders and/or close the entrance by filling the lane with one or more unblocked defenders, or (b) invite the QB to audible – change the call. Not calling the strong-side stretch is a good as stopping it. Preventing the strong-side stretch eliminates it.
  ii. Take away short passing using intense physical pressure to prevent free release by outside and inside receivers.
  iii. Force/invite them to go deep by virtue of the first two objectives.
- In SWAT language, first base/Xpress is communicated with the following call using the SWAT 53 Communication system: 41 – code 14 - 921

After teaching the conventional defensive Diagram (bottom upward), the image is flipped – defense at the top facing downward, showing what the offense sees. This image goes deep – the defense understands the deeper meaning by understanding purpose of alignment and assignment relative to what they are intended to do which is attack the offense, not defend. This is what the offense sees against Xpress. <mark>Diagram 28</mark>

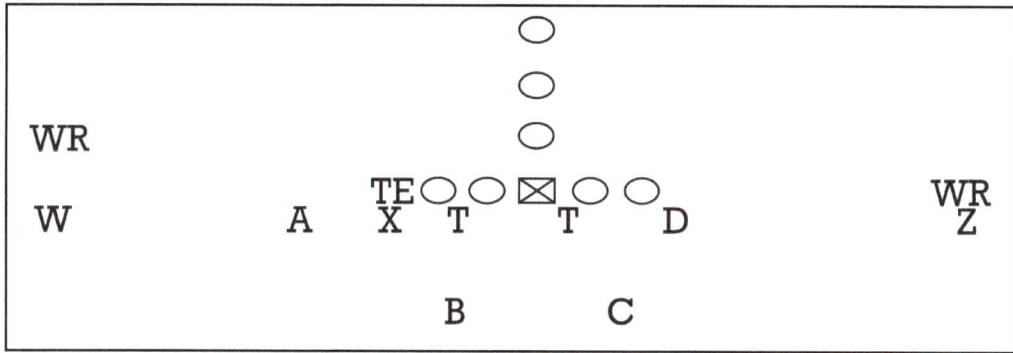

Key points:

- First base is always taught against a 21 Formation – 2 backs and one tight end. This formation is the midpoint between power and spread. Teaching outward in both directions to spread and power is easier than starting at a power or spread formation teaching toward a mid-point.

- The offense sees a 65 pre-snap ratio - 6 in the box, 5 outside the box (space defenders).

- The 6 box defenders are not balanced – the 2 tackles are in strong B gap and inside 1/3 weak A gap but there are 3 on each side of the midline.

- The space defenders are not balanced – they form a 2-3 space ratio.

- The 65 box ratio is misleading. "A" (Alpha), the #4 space defender is the conventional DE, whose sole assignment is rushing the top lane – a 75-degree track that aims to 7 yards behind the right offensive tackle. Alpha never covers in first base – no exceptions, including a back releasing in clear view.

- Alpha's rush track moves him from pre-snap space to post snap inside the box, changing the box ratio to 74 versus the run.

- Versus the strong-side stretch play, A and X (green lines) sprint along the outside and inside borders of the stretch play.

- The distance of Alpha's sprint lane from the trap/kickout blocker is wider than normal. Alpha and the trap/kickout blocker compete in a race, changing the point of impact from where the trap/kickout blocker normally expects. A wrong angle by the trap/kickout blocker guarantees a failed block.

- W, X, Z press the 3 receivers using bench press technique.

- 2 tandems work in tandem. R and Y and B and C have the same jobs: (a) frontside tracking, meaning sprint to where the ballcarrier intends to leave enter the LOS – fill the intended entrance to the running lane; (b) backside tracking, meaning a 30 degree pattern intended to sprint to the midline while spying the ballcarrier to attack any cutback. This 30-degree backside track is the same as the 15 pass pattern (low cross) that is a staple of the SWAT no-huddle offense. The R and Y (2 deep safeties – Robber and Yankee) and B and C (Bravo and Charlie who we call inside linebackers only for point-of-reference teaching purposes because they are required to realign and play multiple positions) are interchangeable. For roster depth, R and Y have the same jobs as B and C. Same assignment, different alignment. Dual-purpose teaching and learning. And, every pursuit angle replicates a common pass pattern in the SWAT no-huddle offense.

- I name each defensive assignment/pursuit angle the same as a pass pattern ie: alpha sprints a 17 pattern. Frontside track from level 4 is a 9 pattern. All defensive lineman run a 9 pattern.

- The A and X sprint lanes replicates a SWAT offense partial pass concept.

- Xpress SWAT 2 lock does not defend…it attacks : (i) strong-side stretch (ii) short passing (iii) invites deep passing. Invites them to think outside the box.

- And it accomplishes the all-important task of building depth by connecting SWAT defense to SWAT offense> By flipping the Diagram, the run defense pursuit angles shows several pass plays.

∞

Second Base

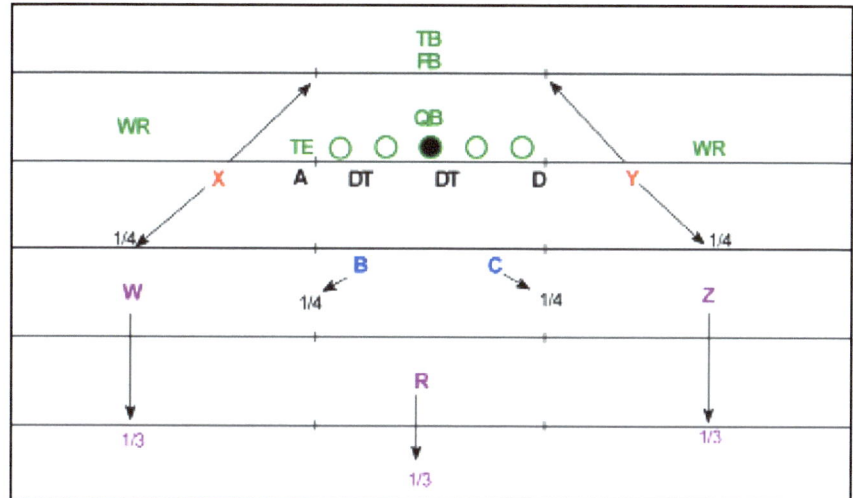

- 2nd base resembles a 4-2-5 zone with an unconventional alignment. 4-2-5 is only a point-of-reference to explain second base to those accustomed to naming defenses with a 3-digit number. But, second base is not a true 4-2-5...or a true 4-3, or a true 3-4. Instead, we call it FleXpress SWAT 3.

- 2nd base is a SPREAD defense, a strongside spread – spread to the single TE side.

- FleXpress means X presses from the flex spot – the slot.

- SWAT 3 means 3-deep 4-under zone

- The box ratio is 65-83 or higher. The offense sees a pre-snap 65 box ratio. Although it starts with 6 pre-snap box defenders, the ratio grows to 8 after the snap versus the run. When the 3-deep defenders enter the box while a run play is in progress, the ratio has the potential to grow to 11-0.

The purpose of the Xpress is the same as first base:

- Take away the strong-side stretch play by occupying both borders and filling the alley with ILBs and deep safeties. X and Y play on a 45-degree track: versus run, 45-degrees on the stretch lane with the intention of shrinking the lane by pushing it back into the box. Versus pass, 45-degree drop to short outside flat zone on the numbers.

- Take away short passing using intense physical pressure to prevent free release by inside receivers.

- Force/invite them to go deep by virtue of the first two objectives.

- In SWAT language, second base/FleXpress is communicated with the following call using the SWAT 53 Communication system: 41 – code 11 – 933

- FlexPress SWAT 3 is a run-stopper because all 11 eyes are looking into the backfield. Additionally, we blitz heavily from this formation, an unconventional approach to zone defense. We rush 5 and 6, shrinking the zone defenders to 6 and 5 because we attack instead of defending. And, we expect zone defenders to match up – coverage starts as zone, finishes in man coverage.

After teaching the conventional defensive diagram (bottom upward), the image is flipped – defense at the top facing downward, showing what the offense sees. This image goes deep – the defense understands the deeper meaning by understanding purpose of alignment and assignment relative to what they are intended to do which is attack the offense, not defend. This is what the offense sees against FleXpress.

Key points:

- Second base is always taught against a 21 Formation – 2 backs and one tight end.

- The offense sees a 65 pre-snap ratio - 6 in the box, 5 outside the box (space defenders)

- The 65 box ratio is misleading. Versus the run, the ratio grows to a minimum 83 ratio because X and Y play on a 45-degree track, facilitating post-snap entry into the backfield box.

- A and D rush inside on a 45 degree track, attacking the inside stretch border. Same effect as first base

- This formation pressures offensive formations that flexes receivers in the slot

- Same frontside tracking and backside tracking rules apply.

- All defensive assignments and pursuit angles replicate pass patterns

Third Base

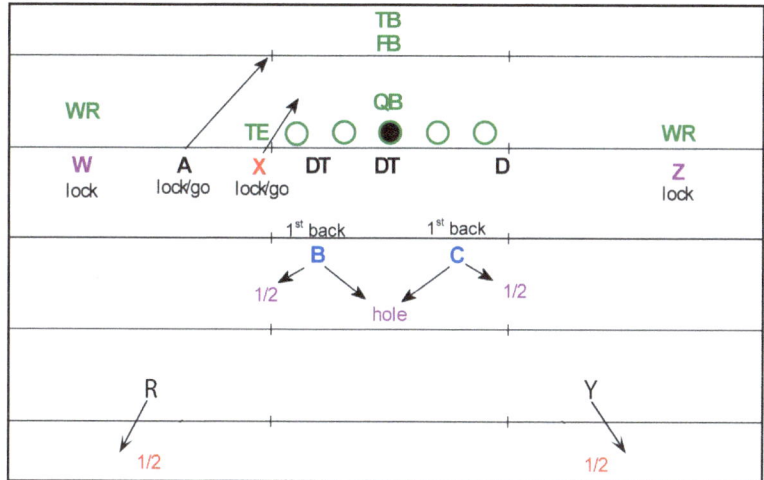

- 3rd resembles a 3-2-6 man with an unconventional alignment. 3-2-6 is only a point-of-reference to explain second base to those accustomed to naming defenses with a 3-digit number. But , third base is not a true 3-2-6...or a true 4-3, or a true 3-4. Instead, we call it AXchange SWAT 2 lock. AXchange is exactly the same as Xpress with one difference – Axcgange has 3 strong safeties instead of 2. Alpha is the 3rd SS instead of DE. A and X always play in tandem on the single-TE side or the left defensive side against double-TE or zero-TEs.

- 3rd base is a SPREAD defense, a strongside spread – spread to the single TE side.

- AXchange means Alpha and X-Ray exchange press/lock duties over the TE depending where the TE is aligned. If the TE is aligned at the inside receiver spot next to the tackle, online or offline, X presses and locks onto TE covering the TE man-to-man while A rushes into the post-snap backfield box.

Key Points:

- SWAT 3 means 3-deep 4-under zone

- The box ratio is 65-83 or higher. The offense sees a pre-snap 65 box ratio. Although it starts with 6 pre-snap box defenders, the ratio grows to 8 after the snap versus the run. When the 3-deep defenders enter the box while a run play is in progress, the ratio has the potential to grow to 11-0.

The purpose of the Xpress is the same as first base:
- In SWAT language, second base/FleXpress is communicated with the following call using the SWAT 53 Communication system: 41 – code 111 – 921

After teaching the conventional defensive diagram (bottom upward), the image is flipped – defense at the top facing downward, showing what the offense sees. This image goes deep – the defense understands the deeper meaning by understanding purpose of alignment and assignment relative to what they are intended to do which is attack the offense, not defend. This is what the offense sees against AXchange.

Fourth Base

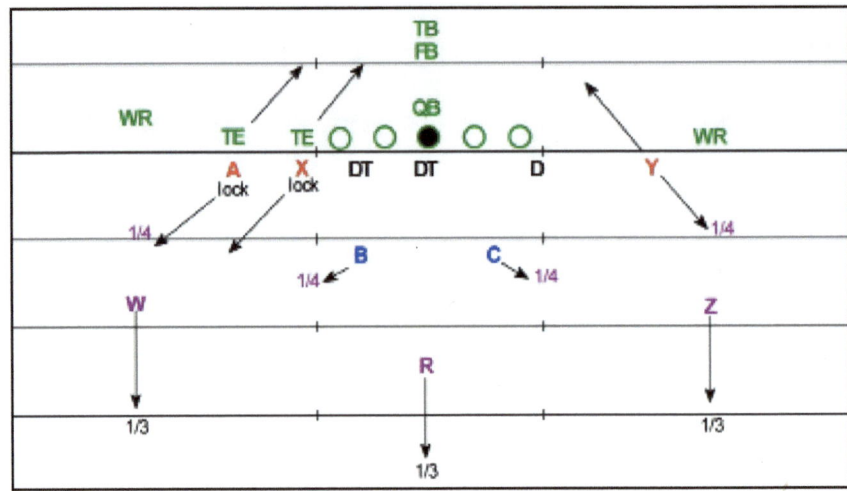

- 4th base is called flAXchange SWAT 3 lock (flex Alpha and X-Ray exchange press/lock duties over TE in zone cover).

- 4th base is a SPREAD defense, a strongside spread – spread to the single TE side.

- 4th base combines 1st, 2nd, and 3rd bases. Three safeties, 3-deep 4-under zone, man press/lock on the TE.

- A, X, Y are the 3 TEs. A and X exchange assignments depending on TE alignment – inside receiver or flex. A and X work in tandem exactly the same as third base – one presses/locks the TE, the other drops to flat zone (short quarter zone).

- In SWAT language, the call is 41-Code 111-931.

- 4th base rushes 3 and covers with 8 but blitzes are always called in 4th base. We never rush only three.

Summary 4 Bases

The four bases represent a sequence – a teaching/learning progression and a strategic framework that fits our reality. The four bases are easier to teach, easier to learn, annually matches our personnel, and connects to our offense in language, assignments, and fundamentals

All four bases are taught against an I 21 formation (2 backs + 1 tight end) for both teaching/learning and strategic purposes. I 21 is the mid-point between spread and power formations. I 21 assignments are the center of the decision-making models to make the call at the line of scrimmage. And, I 21 is included in all of our opponent's playbooks.

Each base is an unconventional formation with a corresponding coverage. The SWAT system has limitless coverages. The 4 bases use only two: (i) 2-deep man/press (ii) 3 deep - 4 under zone. In many cases, these two coverages have been entire game plans.

- 1st base and 3rd base both use man coverage (2-deep man/press). The only difference between 1st and 3rd bas is the number of strong safeties. 1st base uses two strong safeties (XandY). 3rd base uses 3 strong safeties (A,X and Y).

- 2nd base and 4th base are both 3-deep coverages. The only differences are: (a) number of strong safeties. 2nd base uses 2 strong safeties (XandY). 4th base uses 3 strong safeties (A,X and Y); (b) 2nd base uses 3 deep, 4 under zone coverage. 4th base uses the same with man coverage on the TE.

- When 3 strong safeties are used, A and X change responsibilities. When 2 strong safeties are used, A is a DE/OLB.

Players are expected to learn all 11 assignments in all 4 bases – defensive context. It's not enough to know individual assignments. The whole defense – the big picture – has to be understood for six reasons:

i. Raising football IQ. Knowledge is power. Learning only a single assignment inhibits intellectual growth. It keeps players in isolation, disconnected from the intellectual whole.

ii. Rationale. Learning all 11 assignments teaches why we do what we do. Learning reasons deepens understanding.

iii. Making the right call. The SWAT decision-making models work only if every defender knows how the defense works as a whole.

iv. Roster depth. We are not in the NFL. Or D1. Roster depth is a major challenge. Learning the whole defense expands a player's versatility…his capacity to play multiple positions. It breaks limits.

v. Learning the whole defense builds offensive expertise. Studying defense improves offense IQ and vice versa

vi. Playing careers are training grounds for coaching careers.

The unconventional elements of the 4 bases are: (i) the fully occupied TE (ii) the wide flexed/slotted strong-side rusher (iii) the stretch bind created by the fully occupied TE and the wide flexed/slotted strong-side rusher. The stretch bind refers to the blocking decision imposed on lead, trap, or zone blockers (iv) positioning the flat defender on level 1 instead of level 2. The benefit of the level 1 flexed/slotted flat defender is the 45-degree track that positions the flat defender directly on the stretch play track and the track to the lower flat.

SCORES is a problem solving model that emerged from and is predicated on a 5-step rapid-decision-making (RDM) model I developed to teach college law enforcement. RDM is a warp-speed investigative model that works wonder in both policing and football. The goal is to define the problem, then solve it. The problem means the specific intention of that act that the offense intends to execute. It's impossible to solve a problem without fully defining it. RDM defines the problem and solves it on a 3-point EBD continuum - evidence, belief, decision. The secret is gather evidence, form a belief, make a decision - formation + information. Conclusion. Make the call:

i. Formation Recognition. Scan, observe, and build an evidence network based of offensive alignment – temporary and final:

a. Count the backs, TEs, and space receivers

b. note how that formation was reached. Motion and shifts are key indicators of intention.

ii. Classify the formation. Establish the full ratio, the 3-digit number that classifies the type of offensive formation

iii. Offensive Play Recognition. Analyze the full ratio combined with situation and study… what is known about the offense's habits. Predict the offensive call.

iv. Classify the belief. Classify the level of certainty of the offensive call prediction. There are 3 levels of beliefs: (a) reasonable grounds (b) mere suspicion (c) none

v. Make the call. Based on evidence and belief, call defensive alignment and assignments: formation, coverage, and pressure.

Scan, shift, situation, and study > evidence > belief > decision… the call made at warp-speed.

Rapid decision-making makes or breaks defensive coordinators.

∞

Base Call: Defensive STRETCH Play©
41-Code-14, Bravo 1, 921

The unstoppable ground stretch play causes a slow, painful beating.

There are two ways to stretch a defense – horizontally and vertically. Ground stretch and air stretch – force the defense to run east-west and north-south until the defense snaps. When the ground stretch play can't be stopped, you will be beaten into the ground. Stopping the ground stretch is non-negotiable. It's mandatory. Not stopping the ground stretch is disastrous – the game will end up as a lopsided pummeling…slowly and painfully.

When we can't beat your ground stretch with Stile (strength, size, skill, or speed), we use system – the stretch play… the defensive stretch play, to beat the offensive stretch play, beat short passing, and invite deep passing. <mark>Diagram 29</mark>

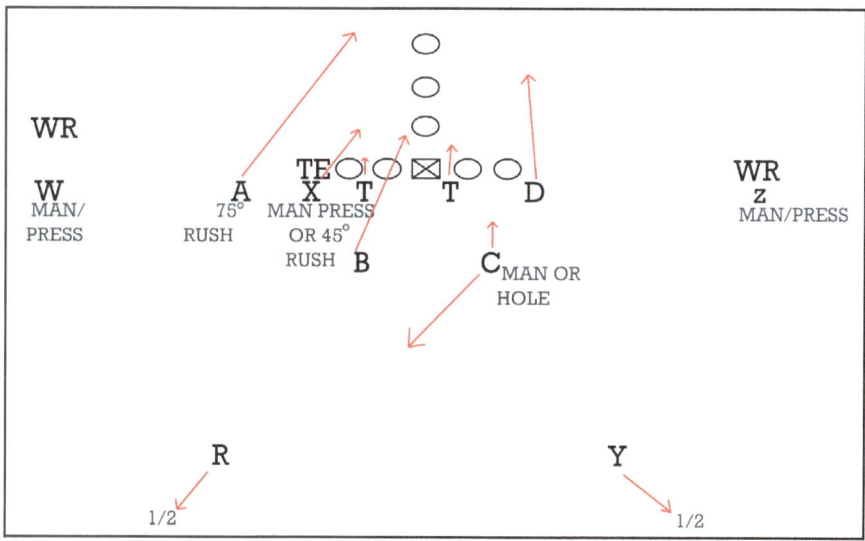

This diagram illustrates the base call of the SWAT system - the defensive stretch play, a unique formation and strategy that features 4-way pressure: 3 presses, 3 robbers, 3 BAA interior rushers, and strong-side blocking bind. The objectives of the defensive stretch play are:

i. stop the strong-side stretch,

ii. stop 3-step short passing, and

iii. invite deep passing.

Stop the ground stretch and force a vertical stretch… that's the primary aim of the defensive stretch play. The defensive stretch play sends a message to the offense: We won't let you stretch to the strongside – put the ball in the air and go deep. We won't lose on the ground even if we mismatched. If you're going to beat us, pass. The farther you try to go deep, the better the chances we have to upset a stronger team.

The defensive play can be:

a. called without a huddle,

b. changed at the LOS with no-huddle, and

c. re-designed into countless derivative formations and derivative plays that achieve the same objectives, without a playbook.

The base defensive stretch play emerges from the Xpress SWAT 2 Lock first base formation but that's not what the defensive stretch play is called on the field. The field call in SWAT language is: **Diagram 29b**

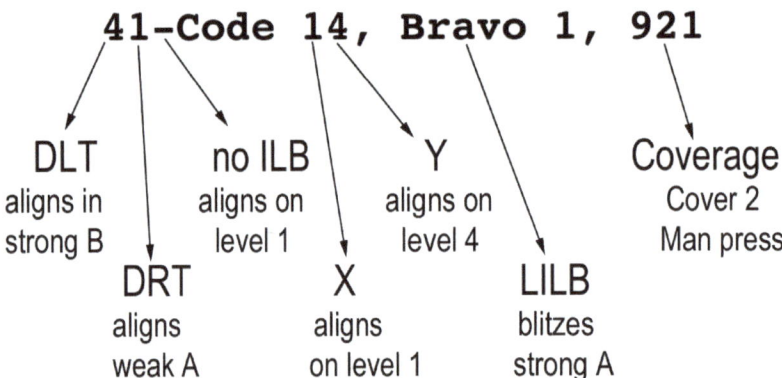

41 –Code 14, Bravo 1, 921 instructs 11 alignments and assignments with 4 out of 5 possible elements in the 53 communication system. Memorization is replace by translation. The 53 communication eliminates all alignment and assignment recall errors. The dreaded mental mistakes have been solved. The 53 communication has fast-tracked teaching and learning.

The 21 left offensive formation is the teaching starting point – 2-backs, 1-TE on the defensive left. That offensive formation is always the starting point for teaching because:

a. it makes most sense for learners. The 21 formation with the TE on the defense's left is the center of the spread-power continuum. Double-TE and zero-TE are included formations, derivatives of single-TE, not vice-versa. All defensive changes form a network that stems outward from single-TE as the core. The 21 offense fast-tracks teaching and learning.

b. despite the spread of the spread offense, single-TE remains the base of most of our opponents.

The Stretch Play features elements:

i. **Occupy the TE**. A strong safety is positioned directly over the TE (nose-nose) and presses the TE on every time the base call is made, trying to break the TE's will – tire him out mentally and physically, make him quit. The benefits of this alignment and assignment are: (a) makes the TE fight the press instead of letting the TE run free as a receiver – hot or deep; (b) forces the TE to earn his blocks (c) positions the SS close to C gap (d) in conjunction with Alpha, binds the blocking scheme. X is a dual-responsibility player – cover the TE or fill C gap at a 45 degree rush angle.

ii. **FleX-man.** Flexed EMOL. Put the strongside DE (Alpha) at the widest end-man position called the 'flex' spot, a minimum of 1.5 yards outside the TE and a maximum of 3 yards. Alpha's only responsibility is a 75 degree rush angle. No coverage, no read. This track has a dual-purpose: (a) it's the outer stretch lane. The FleX-man occupies the intended ground stretch lane. In conjunction with X, the stretch lane is bracketed inside (b) the FleX-man enters the backfield deep, about 7 yards above the tackle, even with the QBs deepest drop.

iii. **Occupy both wide receivers.** Both corners are nose-on-nose, pressing the wide receivers, and locking onto to them. Same concept as the TE press – force them to fight for release and try to break their will.

iv. **Rush 3 into B.A.A. gaps.** It's imperative to pressure strong B and both A gaps with hard blitzes, not simply gap assignments. In the base call, two DTs and the strongside ILB (Bravo) rush strongside B and both A gaps

v. **3 robber triangle.** The robbers drop into zone coverage forming a triangle – weakside ILB (Charlie) drops into the hole; both safeties drop to deep halves. From a QBs perspective, the middle of the field is not clearly open or closed. Neither is the middle horizontal seam that separate deep and short coverage. Versus run, all 3 robbers' eyes are in the backfield, strengthening run support.

The result is a unique way to track the ball: 6+5…65 ball-tracking ratio.
- 6 cover; 3 eyes on receivers + 3 eyes on the QB.
- 5 rusher who defend the run on the way to the QB.
- $3^3 + 1^2$. The base call 3x3x3 and 1x1 distribution; three presses, three robbers, three BAA rushers, one flex rusher, one weakside tight rusher.

The offensive connection. Here's how the defense connects to the offense:
a. same police language is used. Same code words, same digital terminology
b. same communication principles – memorization is replaced by translation. The 53 communication system connects partial concepts into a sentence, just like the SWAT pass play communication
c. formations are the product of instructions – formations don't have names
d. blitzs are called like running plays
e. coverages use 3-digit numbers like running plays
f. flex-man runs the stretch track like a running back
g. X-man plays the TE position – in reverse
h. the low robber closes the middle of the field (MOFC) by running a post pattern
i. the deep robbers close the corners by running corner patterns
j. lock defenders run routes like receivers – in reverse.

Same mind-set, same speech, same skills.

STRETCH Philosophy: Defensive PSYCH101

The defensive mindset is the most important element of: (i) coordinating a defense (ii) executing every play. Like any play call, the Stretch Play is useless without an accompanying mindset to make it work as planned. But mindsets are not created equal. We believe in an attack mindset. Mindset doesn't just happen. Nothing just happens. It has to be developed. Taught. Learned…trained. Teaching the Stretch Play includes Defensive PSYCH 101 – a SWAT philosophy course that every player has to buy into to make it work. Defensive PSYCH 101 is a 20-point program:

Item 1. **The secret to stopping the run: Break the QB's will…Break the receivers' will.**

The aerial-ground connection: to shut down the ground attack, shut down the air attack.

The run cannot be defended in isolation. Neither can passing. Neither passing or running can be defended – they have to be attacked…in sequence.

Passing and running are connected by balls – the QBs and receivers. Fearless QBs, fearless receivers build a fearless ground attack.

Great aerial attack elevates ground attack. The secret to a great aerial attack starts with a fearless rocket launcher – a QB with balls. Not the scheme, not the Xs and Os…the level of QB courage is the starting point to explosive aerial attack. The level of security determines the level of QB courage. A secure, protected QB promotes a fearless QB.

Balls distribution strengthens both pass and run – passing balls to receivers is the second component to the aerial-ground connection. Fearless receivers teamed up with a fearless QB forces the DC and the entire defense to take their collective eyes off the ground game. Just the threat alone of a great aerial attack weakens run defense. A passing threat distracts and detracts from run defense by breaking ground defense concentration.

Removing the aerial threat automatically strengths run defense. Shutting down passing shuts downs running. To ground any aerial attack, security must be broken. Not compromised, penetrated. The secret to coordinating a defense is breaking security…attacking offensive security, not simply defending the offense attack.

The secret to disconnecting the aerial-ground connection is breaking wills. Break the QB's will – break receivers will. That's our primary aim. Break their will to go deep, their will to fight, their will to protect themselves from an onslaught of pressure.

Item 2. **The best coverage is pound and ground — pressuring the quarterback.**

Fearless quarterbacks are the most lethal weapon for any defense. They are explosive weapons, capable of mercilessly bombing any defense at any level.

The best coverage is not man coverage, not zone coverage, not cover one, not cover two, not cover three, not cover four. The best coverage is QB-IMPACT - legally hitting the QB as often as possible. Pound and ground. Pound the QB to the ground, legally. Like in real-life, the goal is to make an impact – on the QB. There are two reasons why pound and ground is the best coverage:

i. Neither man coverage or zone coverage will consistently cover receivers. One-hundred per cent full coverage on every play is impossible. Unless you are coaching in the NFL with a group of elite, all-universe defensive backs and linebackers, there will be at least two open receivers on every pass play where four receivers release. According to our film study and re-defined meaning of open receiver, 50% of receivers, minimally, will be open on every pass play. An unpressured QB will consistently find an open receiver and will destroy any defense, at any level.

ii. Make the QB fearful. A fearful QB is an oxymoron – he no longer is a QB.

Relentlessly pressuring the QB shuts down passing and running for two reasons: (i) breaking the QBs will is a guaranteed solution to explosive passing (ii) the run is stopped on the way to the QB. Attacking the QB attacks the run.

Football is a viscous sport. Don't soften the message, don't soften the impact. The QB has to be subjected to as many hits as possible. QB-IMPACT is the best coverage in football. A fearless QB forces the defensive coordinator to take his eye off the running game. It's the DCs job to make the QB fearful. Otherwise, no scheme will stop the opposing offense.

Item 3.   The second best coverage is roaming charges — pressuring the receivers.

Fearless receivers are lethal weapons for any offense; they are explosive weapons, capable of mercilessly bombing any defense at any level.

Receivers who are permitted to roam freely before and after a reception will become fearless, building up their capacity to gain extraordinary amounts of yardage and score countless points. That's why roaming charges are needed. Receivers have to pay for roaming with explosive hits at one of 2 places: (a) at the line of scrimmage, and (b) immediately after every reception.

Impacts are needed to prevent: (i) free release, and (ii) Z-MAC. Not just yards after the cat, not inches after the catch…zero millimeters after the catch. Press them at the LOS or pressure them immediately after the catch. Although both impacts will instill fear and eventually break the will to catch a pass, the first impact, at the LOS, is the most important. Blocking the receivers first 2 steps will change the nature of the pass play and will stop the pass play from happening as intended – guaranteed.

LOS pressure is more important than the type of coverage. No coverage has the same impact as physically attacking receivers at the LOS. The reason why it fails is mismanaged fear of the risk. The myth of bump and run risk. LOS pressure has a bad reputation – it's labeled as a risk. Any perceived risk causes stress, anxiety…apprehension. Re-define risk. Change the definition, change the outcome. It's not a risk. The real risk is allowing receivers to leave the starting blocks unimpeded and running their race without a single roadblock. That's the real risk.

Item 4.   Connected Pressure — Pressure the run on the way to the QB

There is no difference between run pressure and pass pressure – they're the same. They are not separate concepts. It's impossible to distinguish between pressure intended to stop the run and pressure intended to stop the pass. They are connected because they both are forward sprints. All pressure is forward movement. Defenders who sprint forward apply the same pressure whether the offense attacks on the ground or air.

The blitz myth. The word 'blitz' is a limiting and misguided myth because it builds the wrong mind-set. Players believe that blitz is exclusively intended to defend a pass play. False assumption. There is no such thing a pass-play blitz. Blitz is slang for pressure from a single-responsibility player. It applies to and disrupts both pass and running plays. Blitz is forward movement that reduces the defender's assignment to single-responsibility... attacking the offense by moving toward the LOS and penetrating it into the backfield. The defender is liberated from the complexity of dual-responsibilities. Single-responsibility automatically elevated a defender's performance because it simplifies his job – one assignment instead of two. It doesn't matter if the offense runs or passes. Blitzes have the exact same effect regardless if the offense attacks by ground or air. Blitzes are a ball tracking tactic – search for the run on the way to the QB.

Pressure the run on the way to the QB. Run defense is a derivative of pass defense – run defense is included in the pass rush, not separate from pass rush.

Item 5. Force forces Flight, Freeze, or Fight – In that Order

The concept of pressure applies to both pass and run defense. Pressure is defined as force that forces "in-progress" decision-making; force that forces offensive players to make warp-speed calls during a play - force that forces blocker and ball-carriers to make a call in the blink of an eye. Force that forces a rushed decision.

Great offensive players convert defensive rush to an adrenaline rush. That's the formula for fearlessness. Blockers, passers, runners, and receivers who make this conversion will destroy any defense at any level. But, that process doesn't just happen. No one is born fearless. Fearlessness does not develop overnight. A long road must be traveled. Thousands of reps are needed for offensive players to make that 3-stage transformation, from flight to freeze to fight. That's the strongest advantage for a defensive; during that journey, pressure will make offensive players crack under pressure until they learn how to deal with it.

Like in real-life, pressure cause cracks. Pressure builds mounting stress and anxiety that diminishes performance bringing it to a standstill or slamming it into reverse.

Item 6. Down-Size Dual-Responsibility

Any "in-progress" play has two elements: (i) risk and (ii) uncertainty. Unless you're an expert, doing only one job is hard enough. Two job responsibilities can be overwhelming for any one, especially the inexperienced. All job performance skyrocket when the job description is simplified.

Dual-responsibility players have two jobs, two assignments that require "in-progress" decisions, referring to calls that have to be made while a play is happening. Like any real-life jobs that calls for "in-progress" decisions, there is a steep learning curve dotted with countless mistakes.

The best way to reduce defensive mistakes is eliminating or simplifying "in-progress" decisions by reducing the number of dual-responsibility players. Single-responsibility jobs have a laser-like narrow focus that builds a burning single-minded drive, fast-tracking the road to expertise. After mastery is attained at one job responsibility and monotony and boredom set in, adding dual-responsibility challenges experienced players. Until then, dual-responsibility is an unrealistic expectation for any novice, a daunting task that leads to frustration and anxiety.

Limiting the number of dual-responsibility players unleashes the full potential of a defense.

Item 7. Anticipated Pressure is Just as Strong as Actual Pressure

A real blitz and the threat of a blitz are the same thing, if the threat is real and taken seriously.

Reputation and appearances matter. Consistent heavy blitzing and pressing combined with the appearance of more builds a security threat whether you blitz and press or not. And, security threats create panic, paranoia, and fear.

After offenses experience and compensate for blitzes and presses, they become security-conscious. They raise the security level leading to over-compensation, predictability, and mistake-prone tension. When an offense anticipates defensive pressure, the effect is the same as actual pressure, whether the defense applies it or not.

Developing a reputation for aggressiveness and showing it, makes the opponent expect. Expected pressure is met with chaos. Actual pressure and perceived pressure are the same thing – equal strength.

What you've called before and how you line up is enough to generate pressure, without actually throwing pressure.

Item 8. B.A.A. – The Inside Pressure Points

Three inside gaps, strongside B and both A gaps (B.A.A.), must be pressured with actual blitzes or anticipated blitzes on every Stretch Play.

B.A.A. is a wider midline, an unbalanced 3-lane midline wider on the strong side. The conventional midline is a common point of attack but very few running plays actually stay on the midline during the entire play. The B.A.A. is an extended lane, the place where a large percentage of running plays travel either by design or cutback. And it's the shortest, fastest route to the QB regardless of the length of the QB's drop. Dual-purpose pressure.

The actual or perceived B.A.A. blitz may come from Level 1 or Level 2, and from a 3-point or 2-point stance. The BAA blitz can be any combination of DL or LBs; all 3 from one level or mix of both. BAA pressure is another example of why defensive position titles are limiting and redundant. BAA rushers – doesn't matter if they are linemen, linebackers, or DBs.

There is a dual-purpose for the dual-purpose BAA blitz:

1. Shortest distance to QB. The midline is taken away. Force the QB to leave the pocket. The midline is the natural throwing area. Offline is unnatural.

2. It sets a chain reaction. The offense considers a stretch play to the strong side, where an AX bind that brackets the TE invites a pass or stretch play to the weakside. Exchanging the weakside free safety (Y) to level 2 will send a stronger pass invitation.

Invite them to put the ball in the air. Invite them to go deep. That's the best way to stop the run when you are out-manned up front.

Item 9.   Stretch to Spread

Never try to teach coverage against a spread offense.

Never use a spread offense as the core of the defensive teaching. It won't work. Same rule applies to power double-TE. Don't use double-TE as the central teaching focus.

To teach spread defense, start with the single-TE formation. It makes the most sense for learners because zero-TE and double formation are derivatives of single-TE – they are included formations of the single-TE, not vice versa.

Item 10.   LEVEL 12 and Level 34

Conventional positions are limiting. Tell a young player he's a defensive tackle and that's all he will learn.

Level 12 sends a message to players – you have to move around from Level 1 to Level 2. Same with Level 34. Strong safeties (X and Y) are Level 1234 players. A simple change in language sends a powerful message. Changing job titles from only one level designation to double, triple, and quadruple digits builds an open mind-set. It changes the way players think about defense.

Additionally, it keeps the offense guessing where the 5th rusher will come from – level 1, 2, or 3.

Item 11.   Search and Seizure

In 1984, we taught how to read pass or run. The defense became illiterate, incapable of reading anything. Necessity is the driving force of all change.

We simplified defense, replacing the complexities of reading pass or run with a police investigative concept – search and seizure. Find the ball, get possession of the ball.

Search and seizure is based on proactive ball-tracking, a 5-point plan that governs how each defensive play is designed. We don't try to classify offensive plays as pass or run. We emphasize ball-tracking, as simpler way of playing defense especially with perpetually out-manned open-admission players who are out of their league skill-wise.

The 5 points of proactive ball-tracking are:

    i.   Ground tracking

    ii. Air tracking

    iii. Lock press

    iv. BAA pressure

    v. Flex pressure

All 5 are ways of making "in-progress" observations – conducting a structured search during the play. The first 3 ways are tracking by coverage. The last 2 are tracking by rush.

Our defensive mission is 2 P's – possession and points. Same as offense. Same as special teams. Every unit has the same mission – get/retain possession, score points. This mind-set dramatically changes how players perceive and play defense.

Search for the ball, seize the ball. Get possession of the ball so that points can be scored – by the offense, the defense, or special teams. The defense is expected to score points. Every season, our goal explicitly states that the defense is expected to score at least 2 TDs per game, a radically different stretch goal and expectation but one that has been met and has changed defensive mind-set. Defending the goal-line in not the goal. There are two units on the field who have the same mission – get possession and score. This attitude changes the defenders' perspective of individual and unit assignment from stoppers to scorers. Ball tracking takes on a new meaning, which is to do exactly what the opposing offense is trying to do – score. Even when the defense doesn't score, getting possession for our offense to score is proactive language, as opposed to stop the opposing offense. Changing the language, changes the focus, and changes the outcome.

The 5-point search plan is the simple way of solving the mystery of where the offense will run or throw the football by using our version of the chaos theory: disrupt the offense's intention – change it or stop it from happening.

Reactive ball-tracking is too complicated and too risky. It's time consuming, it needs extraordinary reps by extraordinary-skilled players, and, above all, it allows uncertainty to linger. Offense versus defense is a game of certainty versus uncertainty. The only certainty of the ball's track is from the center to a back - a conventional or unconventional QB, ie. Wildcat. After the snap, the track of the ball is uncertain from a defensive perspective. Whoever plays in the dark longer, loses. That's why the only prevent-defense in the SWAT system is preventing uncertainty from lasting too long. The key is leveling the certainty playing field. The defense must play with equal or greater certainty than the offense – they have to know the path of the ball in warp-speed time; otherwise, the defense will get slaughtered. The defense has to find the ball at the same rate of speed as the intended ballcarrier. Anything slower means explosive offensive plays – over and over again.

Item 12. Ground and Air Tracking

There are only 2 ways to track the ball through coverage:

i. Ground tracking = look at receivers (man)

ii. Air tracking = look at QB's eyes (zone)

These tracking methods don't apply exclusively to pass plays; they apply to running plays as well. Both tracking methods have strengths and weaknesses. The base SWAT call uses both tracking methods equally: 6 total coverage defenders - 3 ground trackers, 3 air trackers.

Item 13. Max Pressure = Lock + BAA + FleXman

Tailbacks used to be MDM on defensive scouting reports - the most-dangerous-men. Not any more.

Stretch plays have the capacity to roll-over a defense. So does interior running. But, stress-free QBs and receivers will do more damage – they can blow up any defense, especially at the open-admission level that we compete in.

DCs can't focus on the tailback and let QBs and receivers operate stress-free. Minimal pressure gives the offense the easy way out – it gives them automatic maximum protection. Minimum pressure is the best security plan for offensive coordinators – not the blocking schemes or all-world blockers.

The base SWAT call uses maximum pressure, that we concretely define as: Lock/press receivers + BAA rushers + FleXman wide rush. Maximum pressure refers to the upper limit of physical force and widest range of geographical force…the most force pound-for-pound from the widest areas. Maximum pressure creates the greatest offensive bind and applies the chaos theory to its highest level.

Item 14. BAA Pressure: One Assignment, Two Outcomes

Stopping the 3-step passing stops the inside run. Two-for-one…dual-purpose assignment. One job, two objectives achieved. It removes the inside run as an alternative to the stretch run, in line with the primary aim of inviting the offense to go deep.

Item 15. Flex Pressure

Alpha has the simplest job in all of football. The single-responsibility of a 75-degree rush is simple to learn and a powerful motivator. Any player can learn it – any size, any shape. And, it helps solve personnel problems. The simplicity of this single-responsibility job increases depth by (i) adding two-way players – every single offensive player can learn Alpha's position, and (ii) rotation – any defensive player (Level 1234 player) can fill in. For example, if you have a surplus of defensive backs who should not be sitting on the bench, rotate them at Alpha. The 75-degree assignment translates to about 50-60 sprints per game. Rotating players into the Alpha position not only is a great fatigue management strategy by keeping players fresh, it's a powerful motivator and developmental strategy. Alpha rotation develops more players than just the 11 starters by meaningfully engaging players rather than excluding them by sitting on the bench. It has generated the greatest internal competition every season – top-speed performance to stand out in the rotation.

We don't use the word 'starter.' We replace it with 'drive # team' – a unit for drive #1, drive #2, and so on. Drive 1 team, Drive 2 team. Routinely, we use the whole defensive roster. In addition to player development, it prevents complacency by build healthy competition for playing time and prevents the toxic attitudes of disgruntled, disillusioned players from rotting on the bench.

What if a RB releases? Does Alpha ever break off his track and cover? No, never. No exceptions. Two reasons: (i) it's impossible (ii) the best coverage is QB pressure. A top-speed sprint cannot change direction and cover a RB sprinting out of the backfield. It's impossible and ludicrous to believe it can happen. Secondly, a charging FleXman has been the best coverage causing the sacked QB or hurried QB.

Item 16   Extended Ground Time + Air Time = Explosive Play Formula

Three factors dramatically increase the capacity for explosive defensive plays called time extensions:

   i. extended 'in-progress' time
   ii. extended possession time
   iii. extended non-possession air time

In-progress time refers to the duration of an entire offense play, from snap to whistle.

Possession time refers to the duration that an offensive play possesses the ball while the play is in progress.

Non-possession time refers to air time - the time the ball is in air. No one has possession while the ball is in the air. On every pass play, the offense voluntarily relinquishes possession. Any play that involves air time constitutes a transfer of possession.

The longer an offensive play takes, the greater the chance for the defensive to achieve the 2P's.

The longer the ball is in the air, the greater the chance for the defensive to achieve the 2P's.

There is a direct relationship between total play time, total air time, offensive mistakes, and explosive defensive plays. Long-developing offensive plays time increases two opportunities for: (a) offensive mistakes (b) defensive big plays. Longer time extensions, the better the chances for a big defensive play – sack, fumble, interception.

Our goal is to invite the offense to call long-developing plays, keep the ball in the QBs hands as long as possible, and lengthen the time the ball is in the air. Extended ground time + air time = increased opportunities for defensive explosive plays.

Extend the QB's possession time and extend air time. The QB is the ball-carrier every second he has the ball, including during his drop, whether or not he has the intention to run. We re-define QB as ball-carrier. He remains the ball-carrier until the ball is in the air. The title ball-carrier gives a different perspective and deeper meaning of offense. With the exception of Tim Tebow-like QBs, the QB is the weakest ball-carrier. And, when the ball is in the air, no one has possession of the ball. A pass is a temporary relinquishing of ball possession – the offense is literally and figuratively putting the ball up for grabs. That's why we call our cover guys receivers. That's why our cover guys must take reps as receivers. Learning to play receiver has been our best training ground for coverage defenders. These concepts dramatically changed our defensive mind-set from a reactionary defensive mind-set to an attack mind-set which increased the volume of defensive big plays.

Changing the mind-set changes the outcome.

Item 17   Make the Offense Defensive

Strategize and Improvise: the defensive play-calling rule. Defensive coordinators face the toughest challenges in the history of football since offensive coordinators discovered that the rules give them significant leeway to line up in wide ranging formations – limitless formations. It's easy to fall into the trap of reactive play-calling – follow- the-leader play-calling…chasing instead of leading. Proactive play-calling controls a team's destiny. Reactive play-calling leads to someone else's destiny.

The key to proactive defensive play-calling is to play your own game. Make defensive calls that puts the offense on the defensive. Force the offense to defend itself. But, the call has to fit the offensive formation. The defense can adjust and match the offensive formation without compromising its leadership role…without surrendering the capacity to play its own game.

Huddle calls are limiting. Huddle calls constitute uninformed decisions. A defensive call made before the offense aligns is only the starting point – a general strategy… a temporary formation that needs a decision to keep or adjust the call – stay in the called formation or go in motion…shift to a final defensive formation after the offense shows its formation.

Strategize and Improvise. As a solution, we connected our SWAT Offense system to the SWAT Defense – no-huddle call with a decision-making model to motion/shift to fit the offensive formation without giving up control of the game. Follow the offense without following the offense.

Call a starting/temporary formation, go in motion to change the formation but keep the nature of the call. Change without change – same as SWAT offense.

Item 18   Make the Wrong Call Obsolete

The biggest myth in football is the notion of the wrong defensive call. Wrong coverage, wrong blitz, wrong front – complete bullshit. There's bad teaching, bad learning, bad skills, bad performance but there's no such thing as a bad call. No exceptions. The concept of a bad call is an excuse that masks bad training and bad planning.

Instead of calls, build a system of moves – decision-making models that cover any situation. Decision-making models make the wrong call obsolete.

Item 19   Physical Fatigue Management

The secret to a winning defense is not Xs and Os. The secret is staying physically stronger longer than the other team – physical fatigue management. He who manages physical fatigue better, wins. The secret to physical fatigue management starts in the gym - the weight room. And, extends to the track. Heavy lifting, hard running. Extreme Physical Strength and Conditioning. Iron deficiency is the leading cause of bad defense. Xs and Os apply what is built in the weight room. But Xs and Os can't save weak, tired bodies and can't compensate for soft bodies.

Weak bodies, weak defense.

Item 20   Mental Fatigue Management

Weak minds, weak defense. The mind tires out long before the body does. Weak minds will beat a defense worse than any spread offense, any power running. Weak minds are the nemesis, the nastiest opponent…the worst enemy known to mankind.

Physical strength is connected to mental strength. The secret to a winning defense is not Xs and Os. The secret is staying mentally stronger longer than the other team – mental fatigue management. He who manages mental fatigue better, wins. The secret to mental fatigue management starts in the gym - the weight room. And, extends to the track. Heavy lifting, hard running. Extreme Mental Strength and Conditioning.

Xs and Os apply what is built in the weight room. Xs and Os organize strong minds, point them in the right direction…unleash the force of strong minds. But, Xs and Os can't save weak, tired minds and can't compensate for soft minds.

Base Play: Making the Call

Another feature that connects the SWAT defense to the SWAT offense is collaborative play-calling. In both the SWAT defense and SWAT offense, the coordinator starts the call and players finish it.

Making the call means applying the SWAT system using a simple 2-step collaborative play-calling process that partners the defensive coordinator and the defensive players by unit:

Step #1   **Build a starting/temporary formation. The defensive coordinator makes the original call. Using the one-page dictionary of SWAT language, the DC builds a 53 Communication sentence, ie: 41 – code 14, Bravo 1, 921…the Stretch Play. The base Stretch Play uses 4 of the 5 possible instructional components. The starting formation also instructs the initial assignments.**

Step #2   **Build a final formation. Players by unit make each make a decision – keep the call or change it. Using the decision-making model, they decide to: (a) stay in the initial formation and keep the initial assignment, and (b) if an audible if needed, motion/shift to fit the offense's formation and match a corresponding assignment.**

The audible decision is the answer to one simple question: Can we run the defensive play called against the offensive formation shown? In other words, Was the right call made? Does the initial call apply? Does alignment and assignment fit. Green light or red light. Go with the original call or stop the original call. No audible or audible.

If the answer is yes we can run the original play – alignment and assignment fit (meaning the right call was made…green light, we can run it – keep the call, it applies) – the play is kept. No audible is called. The green light is communicated on-field with no call – silence. No audible, no additional communication. Saying nothing works effectively. In 1992, I experimented with "green" as a call for the defensive captain to communicate no audible – keep the call. I discovered it wasn't needed. Green was not needed. We learned that the less said is better – faster decisions, greater focus.

If the answer is no, can't run the original play; alignment and assignment don't fit …audible is needed. Red light – stop the original Stretch call. An audible changes the call by re-arranging the Stretch Play. The actual play is not changed…the call is re-arranged. That's the key to fast-track learning and eliminate mistakes. The red light is communicated the same way as with a yes answer – no call…silence. In 1992, I experimented with the defensive captain calling the new play using the 53 communication system. I discovered it wasn't needed. I replaced it with the SCORES decision-making model. Every unit, every player knows what to change. No one has to tell them. Each player makes an observation and knows whether to keep his alignment and assignment or change it. Consequently, we make no call – silence. Again, less said is better – faster decision, greater focus. And we eliminated mistakes.

Step 1 – Original call by DC = 41 – code 14, Bravo 1, 921

Step 2 – On-field decision. Observe and analyze. Does alignment and assignment fit or not? In this case the answer is yes. The call is kept. No audible.

Building the Starting Formation: Assignments

Making the call: Play-calling is a skill. It has to be learned. But, it's not quantum physics. With training, play-calling expertise will be developed if the proper investment is made. As with our offense, play-calling is a shared responsibility where the DC and players work as partners. The key to making the right audible call is understanding when the alignment and assignment fit. Here's how we teach this:

Without a huddle, the DC calls 41 – code 14, Bravo 1, 921. Diagram 31

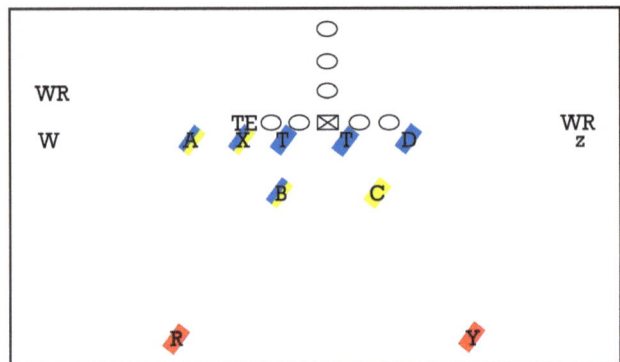

The shaded areas show the unique elements of the formation that confuses the QB:
- blue- shade = conventional defensive lineman
- yellow-shades = linebacker types
- red- shades are safety-types
- Alpha, Bravo and X-ray both have two shades because: (i) Alpha may be a DL or LB-type (ii) Bravo is the 5th rusher – he may be a LB or DL type (iii) X is a strong-safety but looks like a LB-DL type

Formation recognition is impossible.

It's impossible for the QB and blockers to accurately recognize this unconventional formation in a few seconds.

The QB sees an unbalanced 5-2 with 2-deep shell – a false read. Diagram 32

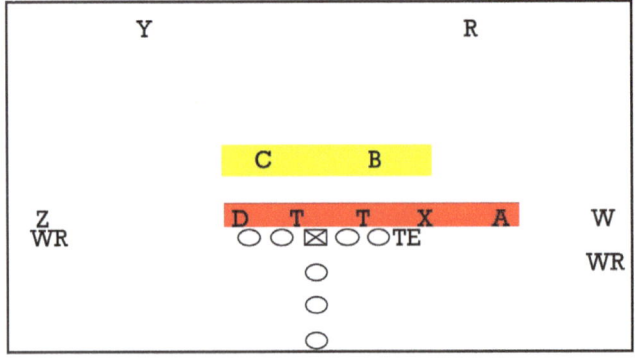

Depending on personnel, the formation can be viewed either a 4-2-5 or 3-3-5. Diagram 33

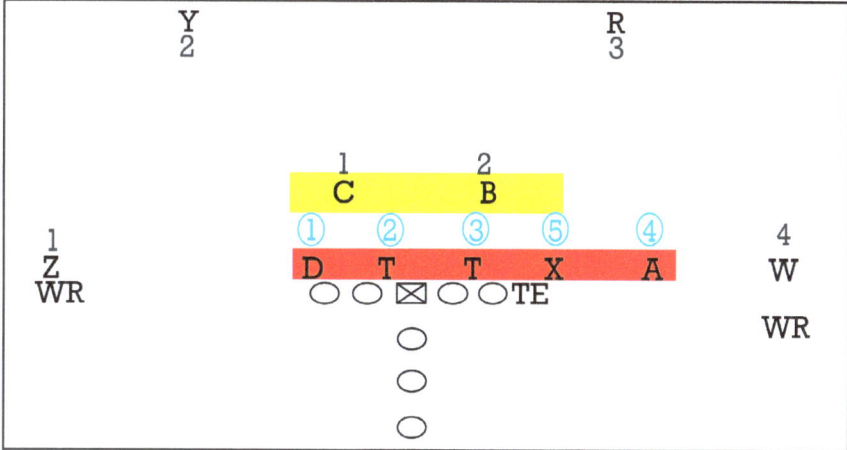

Diagram 34

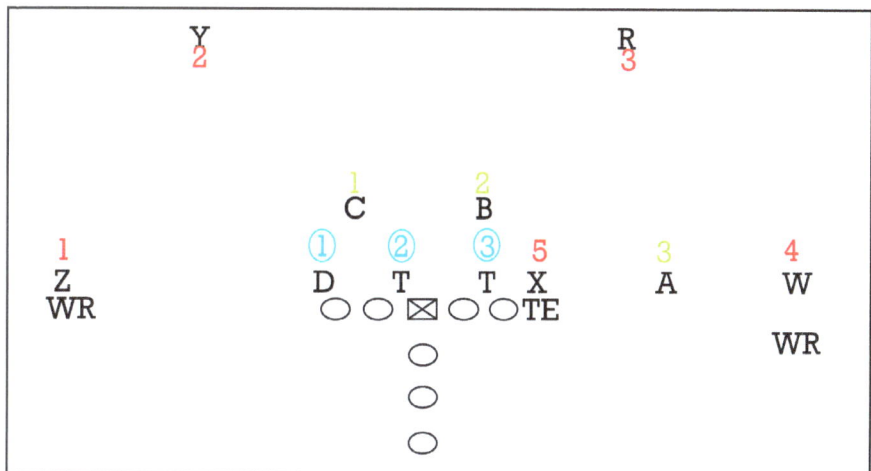

In reality, the formation is a 56 rush/cover ratio: 5 rushers + 6 cover. Diagram 35

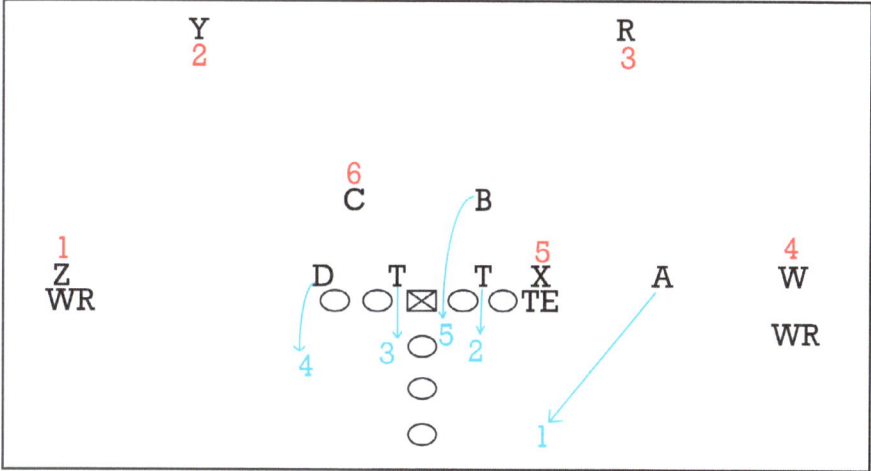

And BELOW, shows a 5/3-3 ratio: 5 rush + coverage is split into a 3/3 ratio: 3 men-press, 3 zone-robbers **Diagram 36**

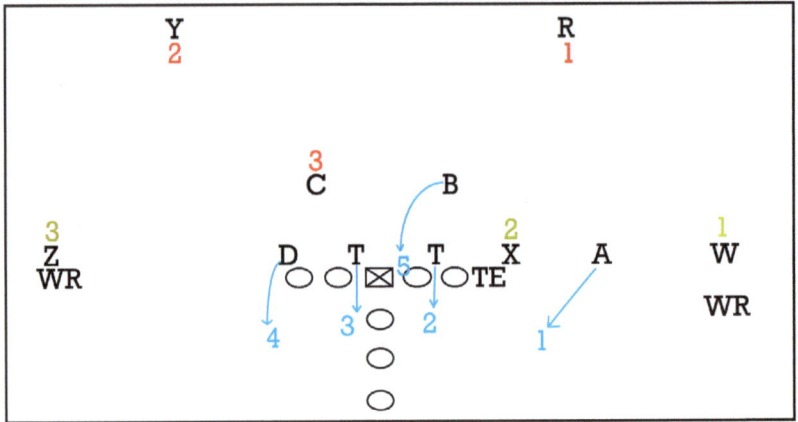

The SWAT XPress prevents three recognitions: (a) formation recognition (b) rusher recognition, (c) coverage recognition. The offense can't count the pre-snap or post-snap box ratio, can't find the number of rushers or the 4th and 5th rusher, and can't recognize the 3/3 coverage ratio split. **Diagram 37**

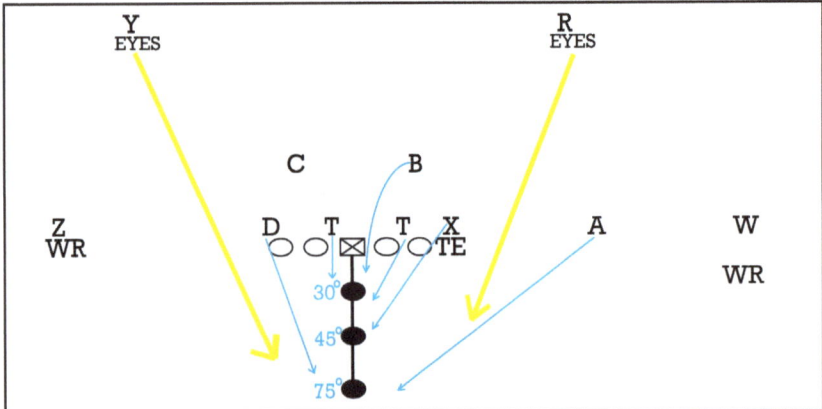

In conjunction with the limitless calls available in the SWAT system, it's impossible to consistently read this defense.

Building the Starting Formation: Translating the Original Call

I have used a wide range of methods since 1985 to communicate the defensive call – manual signals, wristband, messenger - but the absolute best is simply yelling it from the sidelines. The whole defense hears is simultaneously. Then, two designated players, from level 4 and level 2, spread it for good measure: 41 – code 14, Bravo 1, 921 (note: the dash is silent. It represents a blank second element).

Using the 53 communication system (5 maximum elements, 3 minimum elements), the Stretch Play has 4 out of 5 possible components.

Translation:

41:   **aligns the 2 DT's:**

- Both DTs align in 3pt stance in strong B (4) and weakside A-1/3 (1).
- Strong B (4) means the exact midpoint of the guard-tackle gap on the single-TE side.
- Weakside A- 1/3 (1) means nose on the center's outside shoulder, away from the single TE.
- Every gap has 3 points – every gap is divided into thirds: nose on shoulders of the bordering blockers and the mid-point of the gap.
- Assignments: strongside DT penetrate and rush at 45 degrees; weakside DT, penetrate and rush at 30 degrees.

Dash between 41 and code 14: aligns the ILBs (B and C):

- The dash separating 41 and code 14 means 'no LB exchange" – no LB realigns to level 1. This means both Bravo and Charlie align on Level 1, equally-spaced - nose directly in B gaps at a 4 yard depth.

Code 14:   **aligns 5 players - SS (XandY) directly, 2 DE's (A andD), and free safety (R):**

Code 14 aligns the two strong safeties directly and the DE's (Alpha and Delta) and free safety (Robber) indirectly:

- X aligns on level 1, locked onto the single TE – one the LOS, nose-on-nose – on left or right side – wherever the single TE aligns.
- Assignment: vs pass: lock on the TE in press-man coverage; vs. run C-gap (bench press and 2-step C-gap attack - 1st step step to C with inside foot 45 degrees into C-gap; 2nd step and uppercut).
- Y aligns on level 4, at weakside slot/flex: 10 yards depth at the slot/flex spot – the mid-point between the weakside tackle and wide receiver. Assignment: Run-stopper first. Eyes in the backfield, recognize run or pass on first two steps. Versus run: frontside pursuit to the ball, backside pursuit parallel to the LOS. vs pass – deep ½ right side.

- Alpha aligns wide on the strongside, 3pt stance, 1.5 yards outside the TE (wider the better, never closer to X), tilted at 75 degrees. He sprints the highest entry track, a 75 degree angle that aims at back level behind the TE. There are 3 entry points that apply to all defenders, each corresponding with QB drops:

    - 75 degree to 7-step drop
    - 45 degree to 5-step drop
    - 30 degree to 3-step drop

- Assignment: rush at 75 degrees – no coverage. No exception. Alpha never breaks away from his track/assignment. No athlete sprinting at full speed can change directions to leave a 75-degree rush lane to properly cover a RB. If he can do it, he wasn't sprinting at full-speed. Our goal is to minimize dual-responsibility players and minimize 'in-progress' decision-making. We want to reduce the number of players making a call during a play.

- Delta aligns on the weakside, 3pt stance, at one of two places: (i) tight: nose at .5 yards outside the tackle (ii) or flex: 1.5 yards minimum. Both aim for a high spot (7 yards) behind the tackle. The tight alignment makes it harder to get there because the tight rush starts at 90 degrees and maneuvers to 75 degress. The flex alignment facilitates the 75-degree rush. Additionally, the flex coverage binds the blockers – Delta is usually unreachable by the tackle. The weakness with a flex alignment on the weakside is a mismatch caused but the OT blocking Charlie and a FB on Delta, if Delta has not yet developed adequate physical strength, which is very possible in open-admission teams. The alignment decision is situational. It depends on who the opponent is and who Delta is. Their habits combined with our strengths/weaknesses.

- Delta's assignment: rush – no coverage ever.

- Robber aligns on Level 4, at strongside slot/flex spot: 10 yards depth at the slot/flex spot – the mid-point between the TE and wide receiver. Assignment: Run-stopper first. Eyes in the backfield, recognize run or pass on first two steps. Versus run: frontside pursuit to the ball, backside pursuit parallel to the LOS. vs pass – deep ½ left side. **Diagram 38**

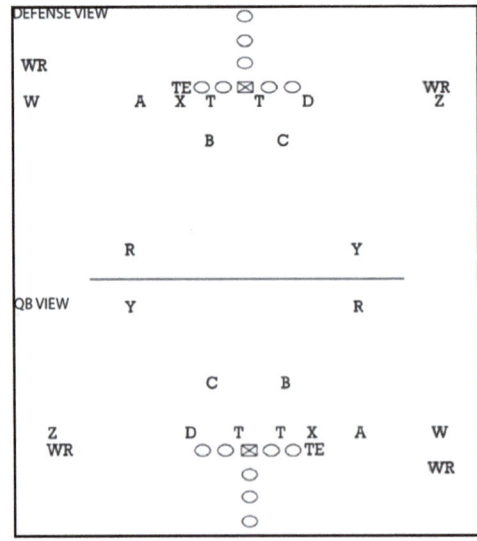

Key Points:

- Bravo 1 means the left ILB blitzes through the left A gap – strongside A. assignment: align at 4 yrads, nose in B gap, entry A gap, and rush at 30 degrees.

- Charlie assignment: align at 4 yards, nose in B gap. Assignment: vs pass: 1st back or drop to hole; vs run, weakside B gap and parallel weakside pursuit.

- 921 means "the coverage is" (9), cover 2 (2), man-press (1).

- W and Z align on the LOS, nose-on-nose. Assignment: bench press and lock in man coverage.

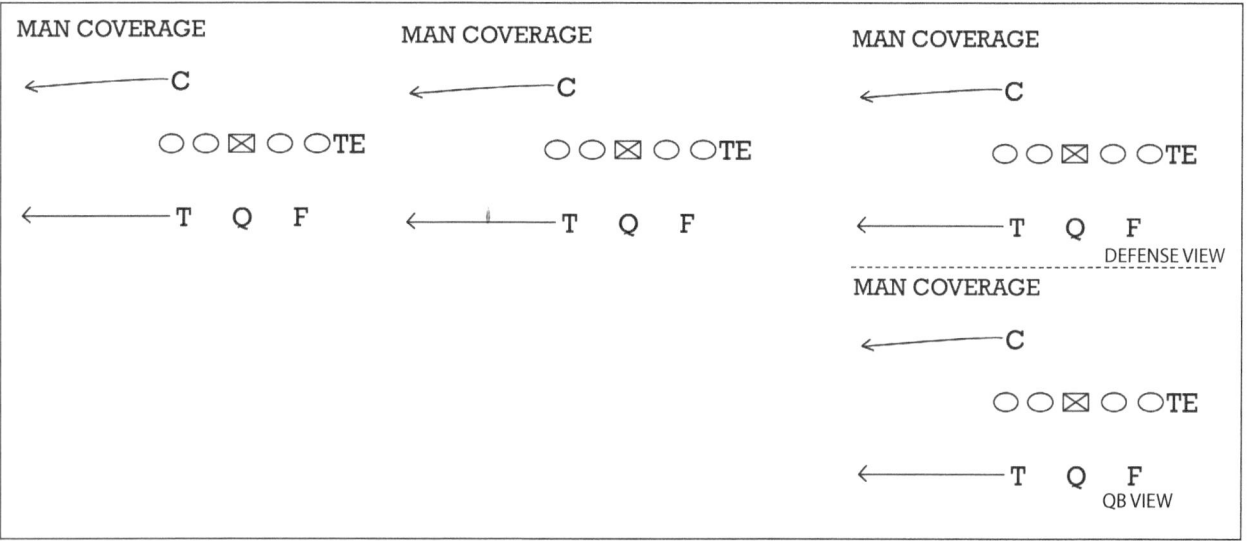

921: Alignment and Assignment Chart

ALIGNMENT	ASSIGNMENT
- W & Z: on LOS, nose-on-nose on #1 WR.	>> Close bench press, prevent free release.
	>> Man coverage; run support = frontside – to the ball; backside, pursue to back of end zone.
- X on LOS, nose on TE	>> Close bench press.
	>> Man on TE. If run, strong C by ripping with outside shoulder.
- R & Y 10 yards at slot/flex spot	>> Run-stop first – frontside to ball, backside parallel pursuit. Pass: deep halves.
- Charlie 4 yards, nose in B gap	>> Run = weak B gap. Pass = 1st back or drop to hole.

Diagram 39

```
WR                                               WR
         TE ○ ○ ⊠ ○ ○
W         X                                       Z
MAN /    MAN /                                   MAN /
PRESS    PRESS            C                      PRESS
         LOCK


         R                          Y
```

Objectives: The reasons for using this base (41-code 14, Bravo 1, 921) against that offense (I 21 left) are:

i. Both formations are the best points-of-reference for contextual teaching.

ii. I 21 left is the base for many of our opponents

iii. All adjustments are included from these formations, not vice-versa. All conversions stem outward from this base.

iv. The BAA blitz is the central feature of the Stretch Play.

BAA Blitz
Key Points

3 BAA rushers simultaneously threaten the QB and cancels midline runs attacks while binding interior blockers. Adding a strong-side B gap rush builds imbalanced interior pressure. Double-A gap blitz are the shortest distances to the QB. Rushing double-A clogs the midline and it forces the offense to declare it's blocking schemes are play-calling early in the game.

This type of BAA blitz has staggered entry times because one defender is leaving from level 2. Strong A entry happens about one second later. After recognizing the efficiency of the blocking scheme, a decision is made to keep blitzing strong A gap from level 2 or show it by re-positioning Bravo on level 1, directing in strong A gap.

We have studied miles/kilometers of film to learn the difference between aligning the weakside DTs directly in weak A gap or nose on center's shoulder. The difference depends on the opponent. Center-shade works if the center is physically weak or the left guard's zone blocking skills are weak. Aligning directly in the gap works if the blocker's first lateral step is slow and cannot close the gap by fully occupying the gap rusher.

Alpha and X-Ray build a blocking bind by the angles and width of their rush. The combined effect of a wide 75 degree rush and a 45 degree rush from the TE's nose is the most unconventional bind that blocker's will ever experience. This bind stops strong side stretch plays by occupying the 2 stretch tracks on the way to the QB the force of the 5 man rush is unbalance, favouring the strong-side. 3 presses: Three receivers are pressed at the LOS.

Robber and Yankee are run-stoppers first, pass defenders second.

three robbers form a triangle versus pass – one in the hole, two deep outside the has marks. This 3-robber configuration defends against scrambling/running QBs and, in conjuction with 3 presses and 3 BAA rushers, is the best way force turnovers because of a decision-making chain-reaction: (a) short passing is disrupted (b) deep passing is invited (c) the capacity for explosive defensive plays dramatically increases when the offense goes deep – QB sacks, fumbles, and interceptions.

Explosive Play Formula

Three factors dramatically increase the capacity foe explosive defensive plays:

i. the longer a pass is 'in-progress

ii. the longer the QB has possession of the ball

iii. the longer the ball is in the air

3+3+3= -3 Rule

3 presses + 3 BAA rushers + 3 robbers = minus 3.

W X Z   D T/B   C R Y

Minus 3 means disrupted 3-step drop which invites deep passing. Diagram 42

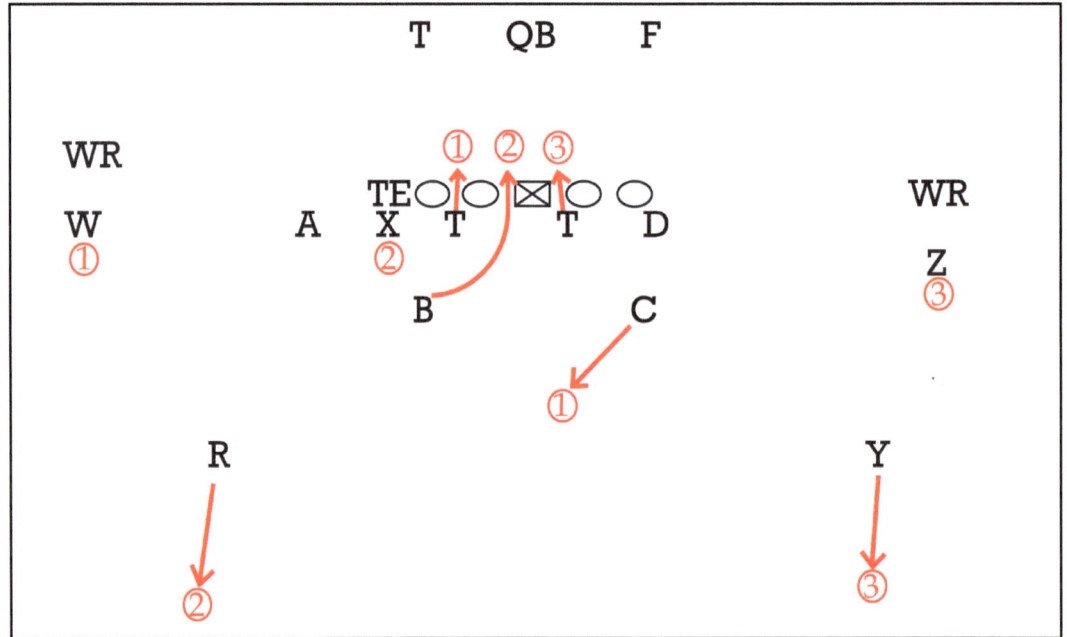

∞

Building the Final Formation:

Defensive Motion/Shift

    After the original Stretch call is made, an on-field decision determines if the right call was made. Step #2 decides whether to re-arrange the call or not. This decision is made by applying the SCORES model. The purpose of the SCORES model is to decide whether alignment and assignments have to change. Additionally, we use it to make no-huddle calls after the offense aligns.

SCORES: Decision-Making Models Alignment and Assignment Conversion Chart

Two general rules govern our decision-making – how to make a call:

Rule #1: Play your own game.
Rule #2: Customize calls that play your own game.

These two rules are two decision-making goals achieved by:

1. See the whole board, know the situation, make the call, remember it. The pre-snap and post-snap read formula, a theory of how to read the offense before and after the snap to recognize intention.

2. Seeing the whole board means see the context – the big picture. Past knowledge including data, patterns, and habits recognized during film study, and 'in-progress' game analysis.

    The theory of 'seeing the whole board' starts with classifying the offensive formation.

    Offenses are divided into classifications by ratio of numbers of TEs, backs, and receivers-outside-the-box(ROTB) space receivers.

This classification chart has 5 columns:

i. # of backs

ii. # of tights end

iii. Back-Tight end ratio

iv. # of ROTB

v. Full ratio – a 3-digit number that equal 5 (number of receivers) –

   - digit 1 = # of backs.

   - digit 2 = # of TEs.

   - digit #3 = # of ROTB

Backs	TEs	RB-TE ratio	ROTB	Full Ratio
2	1	2x1 (21)	2	212
2	2	2x2 (22)	1	221
2	0	2x0 (20)	3	203
1	1	1x1 (11)	3	113
1	2	1x2 (12)	2	122
1	0	1x0 (10)	3	103
Zero	1	0x1 (01)	4	014
Zero	2	0x2 (02)	3	023
Zero	0	0x0 (00)	5	005

Conversion Chart

When the Stretch Play is called: 41 – code 14, Bravo 1, 921, the following 10 simple rules govern all audible/changes that re-arrange the play:

1. twin receivers + single TE (WRs on same side opposite from TE):

    - cornerbacks cover receivers - #1

    - cornerbacks cover twins - when #1 moves to #2 on twin side with or without motion

    a) if WRs shift/motion, cornerbacks chase. Coverage does not bump over. Diagram 43

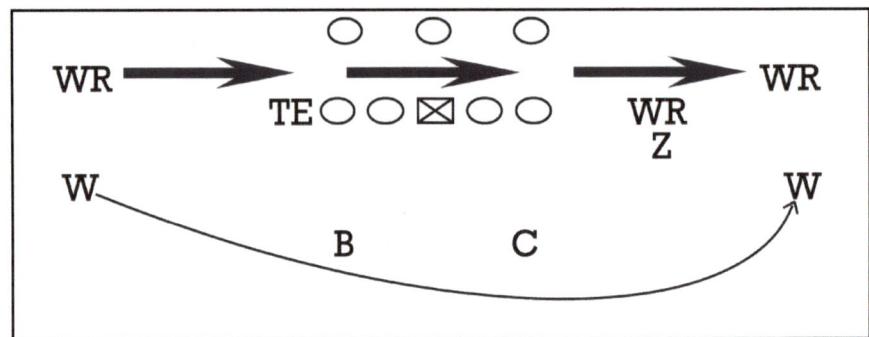

    - chase above the box, not through it. Then, align nose-on and lock on the receiver. No change in assignment.

    b) same rule when receivers align on the same side from the huddle instead of motion – cornerbacks always cover receivers. Diagram 44

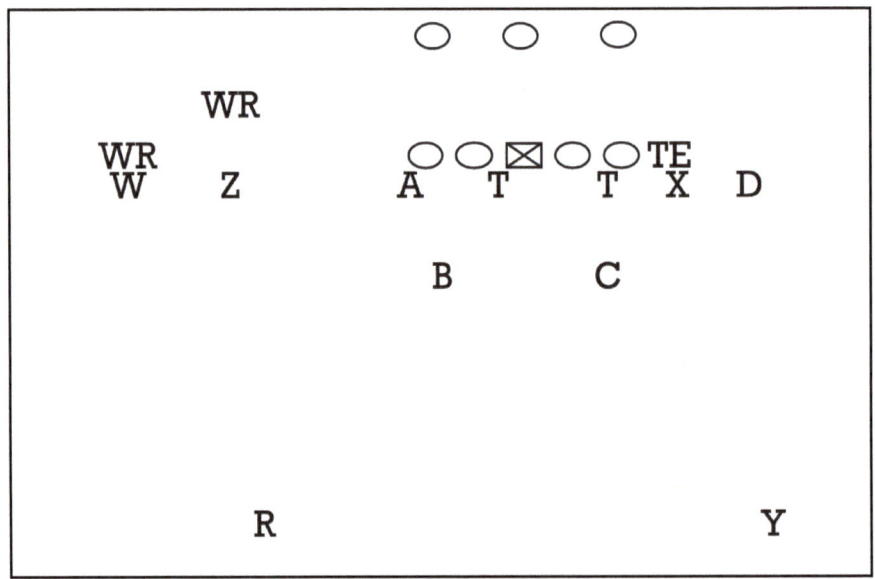

2. X covers single TE, regardless of what side TE aligns on and regardless of number of backs. The DE on the TE side flexes.

3. #4 receiver – with or without shift/motion: convert to cover 1 by FS covering #4. (a) If motion, FS on side of the 4th receiver drops down to cover 4th receiver without pressing - nose-on @ 5 yards. (b) If no motion, Y covers 4, R becomes the midline FS. No other assignments change.

**if RB motions outside the box to WR, LBs do not chase/re-align.

4. #5 receiver = convert to cover zero/no press and rush 6. Second FS covers #5. All DB 5 nose-on, 5 yards off. CHARLIE BLITZES to generate max pressure – 6-on-5

5. Double TE = SS + CB exchange. Both SSs press + lock (X on defensive left, Y on def. right), cornerback replaces Y on level 4 + double-flex DE, except when the DT aligns at NT. Never leave 2 uncovered OL side-by-side.

6. If zero TE = X covers #2 as a level 3 SS + no DE flex – DE on OT's outside shoulder

a) if 2 backs, X covers #2

b) if 1 or zero backs, X covers #2 on defensive left. Diagrams 45

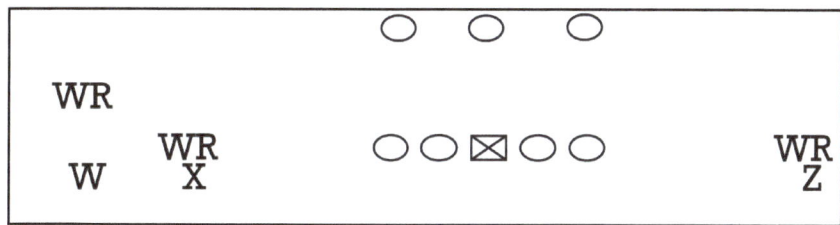

Diagram 46

7. DT exchange: (a) 41 to strongside in single TE (b) 33 if no single TE; if double TE, or zero-TE, both DTs realign to nose-on-guard (33) and both DTs are assigned double A-gap with 30-degree rush (first step to A-gap midpoint and uppercut) – 6 run defenders aim at 3 pressure points. In double-TE, Bravo and Charlie still align in B gap but Bravo exchanges blitz lane from A to B, to maintain BAA blitz;, Charlie has dual-responsibility (B to RB/hole).

8. If single-TE aligns left, the call reverses sides - exchanges: DT exchange alignments; they align 41 to TE; Bravo and Charlie exchange assignment; Alpha and Delta exchange flexing.

9. If RB releases, Charlie covers him man-to-man.

10. If single-back shotgun aligns on Bravo's side, Bravo and Charlie exchange assignment – the ILB opposite to the single shotgun back blitzes strongside A gap.

Summary

- 2 backs: corners cover #1, X TE/#2

- 1 back + 1 TE: WandZ = #1 or twins; X = TE, y=#4

- 1 back + 0 TE: same except X = #2 left side

- zero backs = combine all 10 rules

Audibles: Applying the SCORES Decision-Making Model

Making an audible call by applying SCORES is connected to knowing offensive theory. And offensive theory is connected to the rules of the game. Nothing can be taught in isolation.

It's impossible for players to fully understand the SCORES decision-making model without knowing offensive theory and the rules that govern offensive theory. Every pre-season, I start with a quiz, a simple, elementary quiz that the majority of collegiate-level players fail. This quiz has never averaged 100%. In fact, it's never averaged 50%. It's shocking how many players graduate from high school not knowing the answer to the following questions. It impossible to play defense, understand defense, and make the right calls without knowing the following rules:

Question #1. In both the USA and Canada, what is the minimum number of players that must line up on the LOS?

Less than 50% get the right answer – 7. Seven online-players is mandatory in both countries.

Question #2. What is the maximum number of online players?

There is direct maximum rule. Indirectly, the number in the USA is 10, Canada, 11. The entire offense minus one can align on the LOS. One player is needed offline to receive the snap.

Question #3. Which online receivers are eligible to receive a pass?

The last online man (end) on each side of the line. Two online receivers are eligible regardless if the minimum and maximum number of online players are on the LOS. This means that all the online players between the ends are ineligible receivers.

Question #4. Is a TIGHT end mandatory?

Of course not but this needs to be stress. The ends may align at any place between the tackle to the sideline. This answer has never been obvious to players.

Question #5. In addition to the ends, who else are eligible receivers?

Offline receivers, defined as any player who aligns at least one yard behind the LOS.

Question #6. If there are 7 online receivers, how many total eligible receivers are there?

6 in the USA .

7 in Canada. Subtract 5 from the total number of offensive players. The QB is eligible. Not counting the QB, subtract 6; 5 in the USA, 6 in Canada.

Question #7. What players can realign before the snap?

USA: unlimited shifts, limited motion – one offline player, parallel or away from the LOS.

Canada: limitless motion: This is a nightmare for Defensive Coordinators. All offline players can move in any direction before the snap. If that wasn't enough, the rules were amended to allow the ends to motion toward the ball on the LOS. Combined with the width of the field, it's impossible to cover all receivers, all the time. That's why QB pressure is the only way to stop the pass.

Question #8   What is the difference between shift and motion?

In the USA, motion means pre-snap movement at the time of the snap. Shift is pre-snap movement up to 1 second before the snap. Unlimited receivers may shift in any direction, before the 1 second time limit. This means that an online-offline exchange may occur. However, motion is limited to one online player; unlike Canada, motion is prohibited toward the LOS.

Question #9   What is the number of mandatory stationary offensive players at the time of the snap?

USA: 10   Canada: 5 (Theoretically, the QB can me moving backward at the snap).

Question #10:   How many DEFENSIVE players have to be STATIONARY at the time of the snap?

Zero – on both sides of the border. The entire defense can legally in motion at the time of the snap. The entire unit can be moving. Makes you wonder why defensive players are stationary? What is the point of a stationary defensive target, particularly in the box?

Conclusion: There are limitless offensive formations. The eligible receivers can use every inch online from tackle to sidelines and every inch behind the minus-one yard-line behind the LOS – any depth, any width.

The entire defense must pass with 100% on this test to fully understand defense and to fully understand how to make calls – original calls and audibles. After scoring 100%, SCORES is put in motion – it's taught step-by-step, shift-by-shift to make the Stretch Play all fit any offensive formation. The following Diagrams represent the teaching plan.

Audibles: Applying the Conversion Chart

When the play call is 41-Code 14- 921, the Conversion Rules change the base call to adapt to any offensive formation. Here are examples:

212 Right Diagram 48

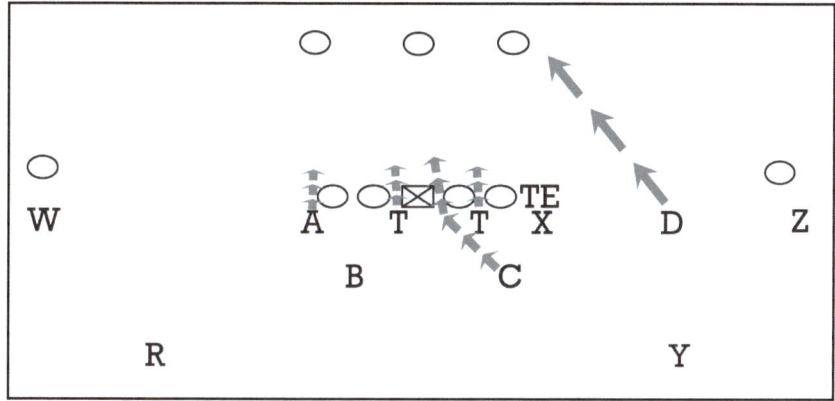

221 Left Diagram 49

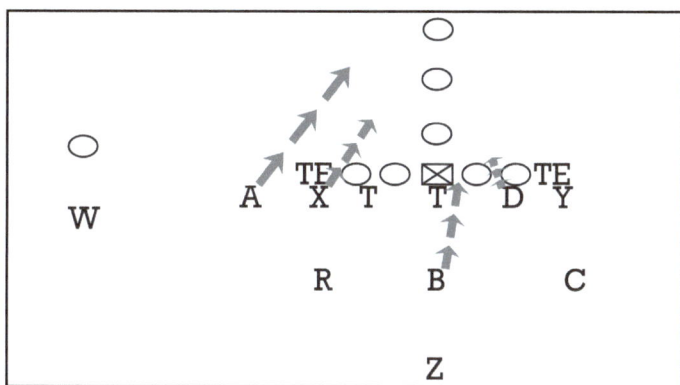

221 Right Diagram 50

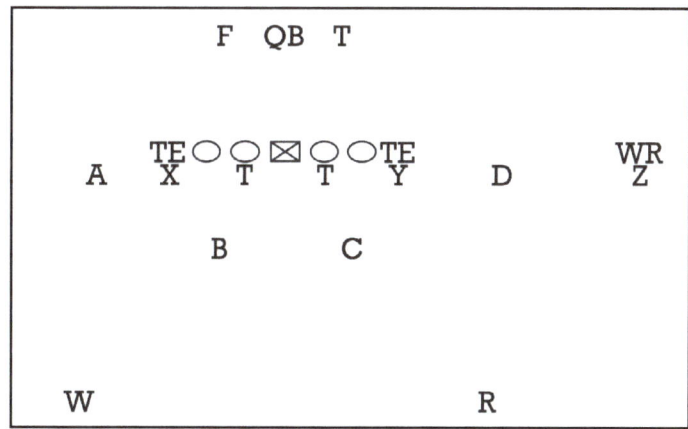

203 Left Diagram 51

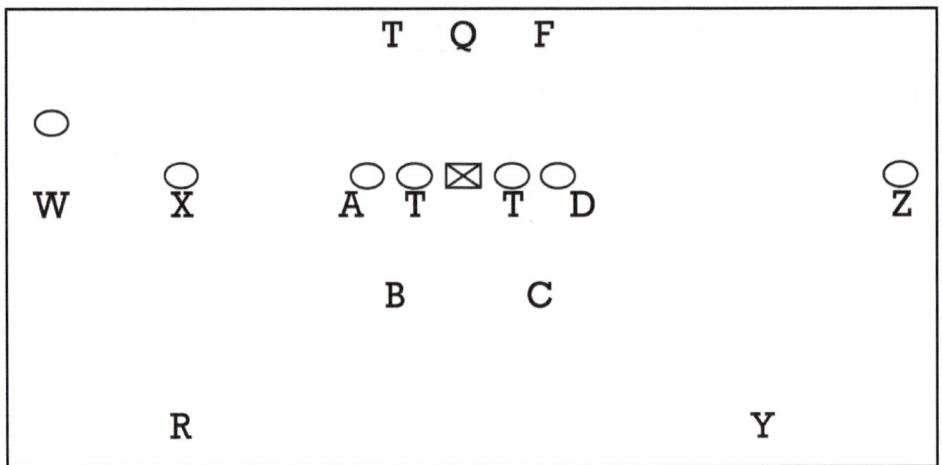

203 Right Diagram 52

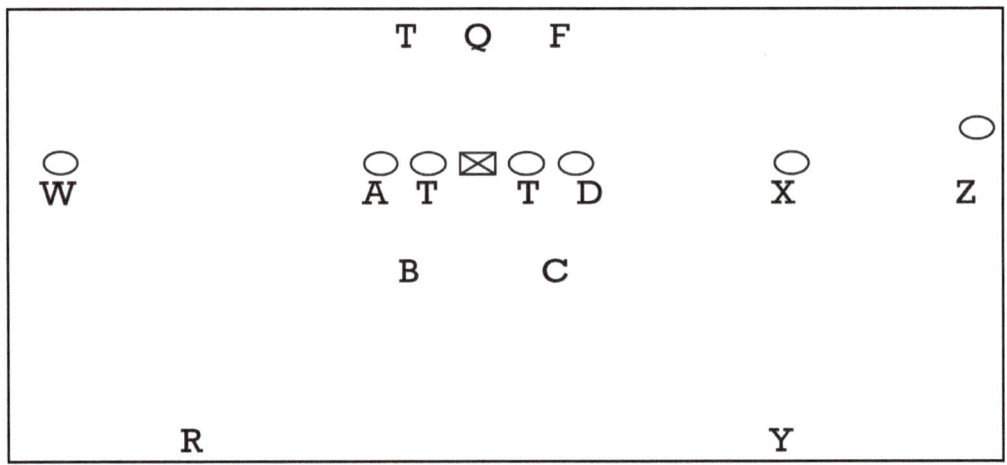

113 Left (2x2) Diagram 53

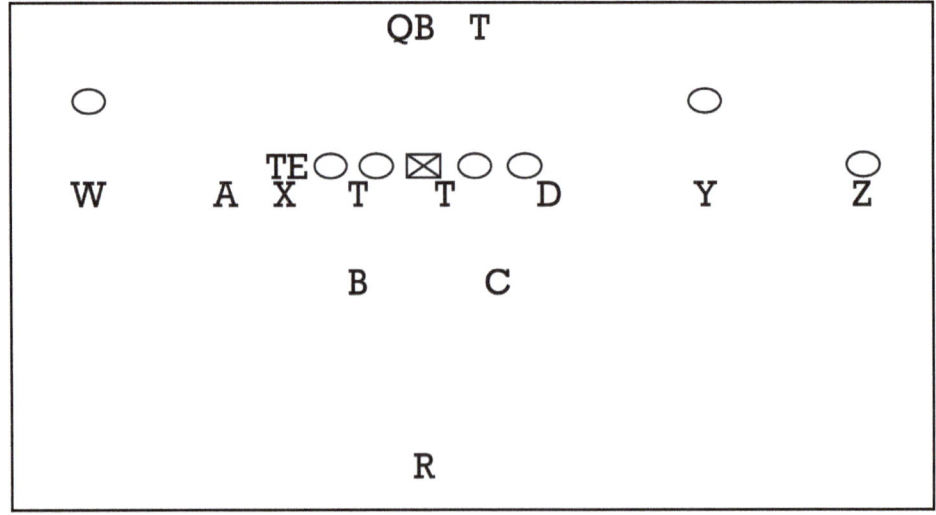

113 Left (3x1) Diagram 54

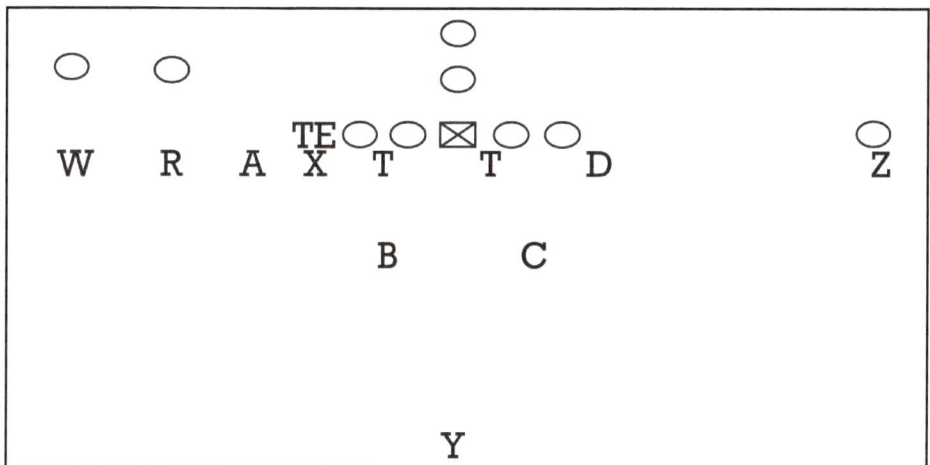

113 Right (1x3) Diagram 55

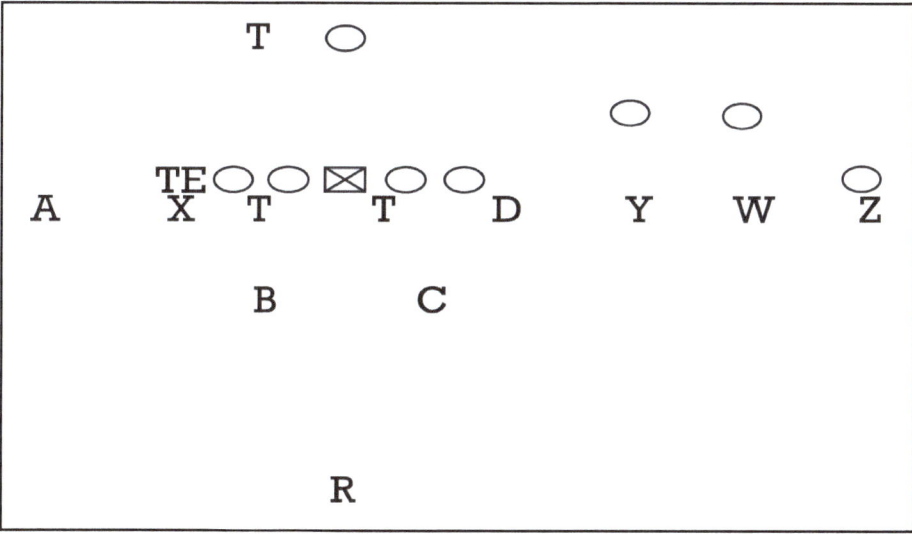

113 Right (2x2) Diagram 56

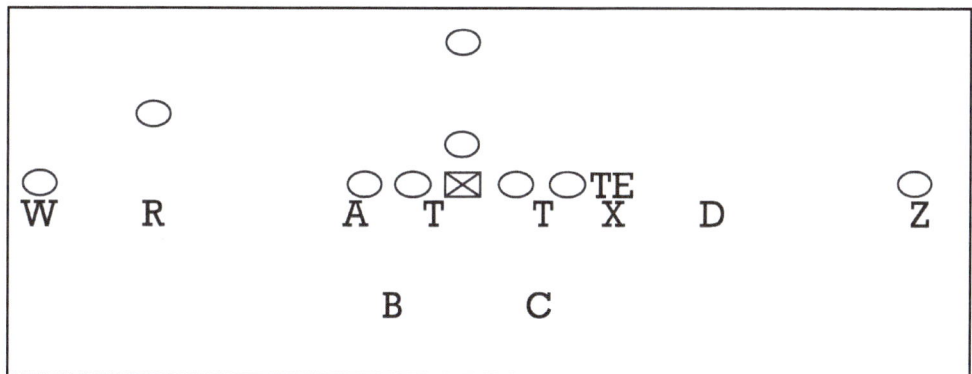

113 Right (1x3) Diagram 57

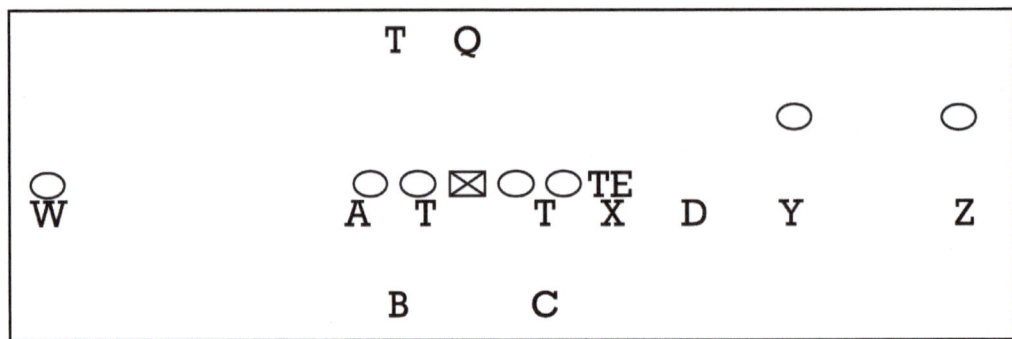

113 Right (3x1) Diagram 58

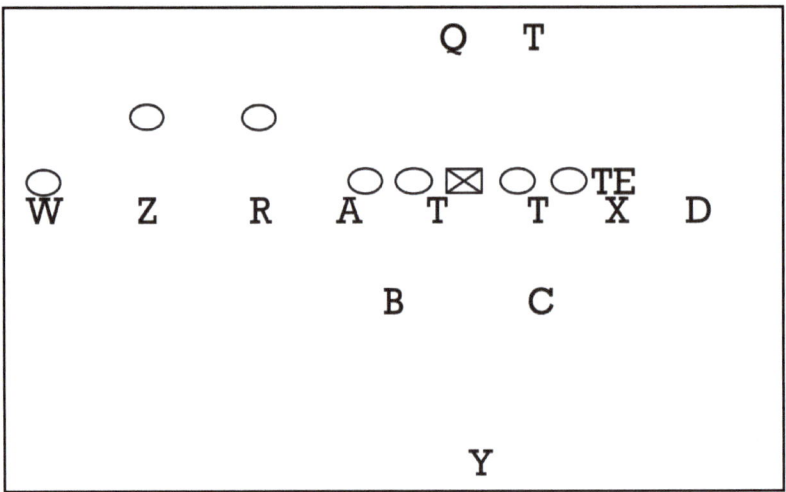

113 Diagram 59

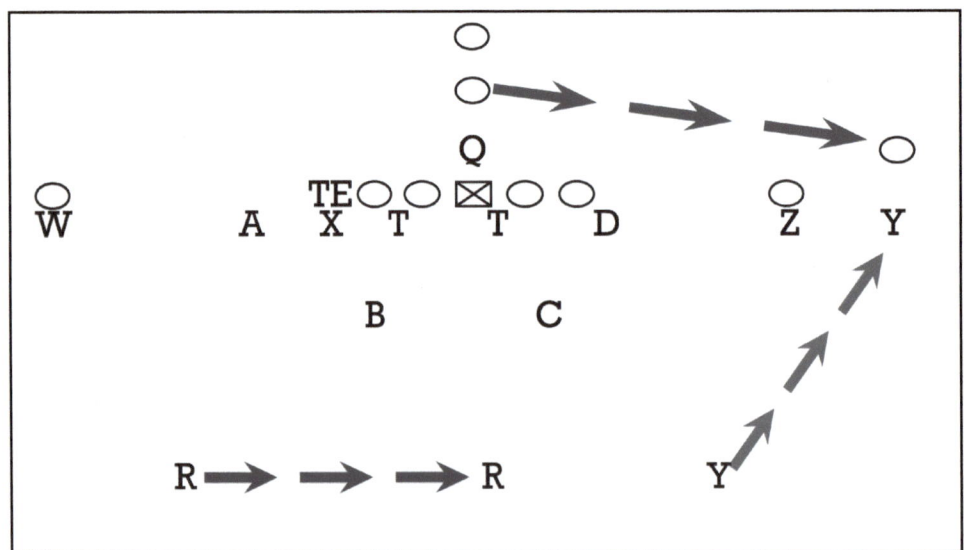

Diagram 60

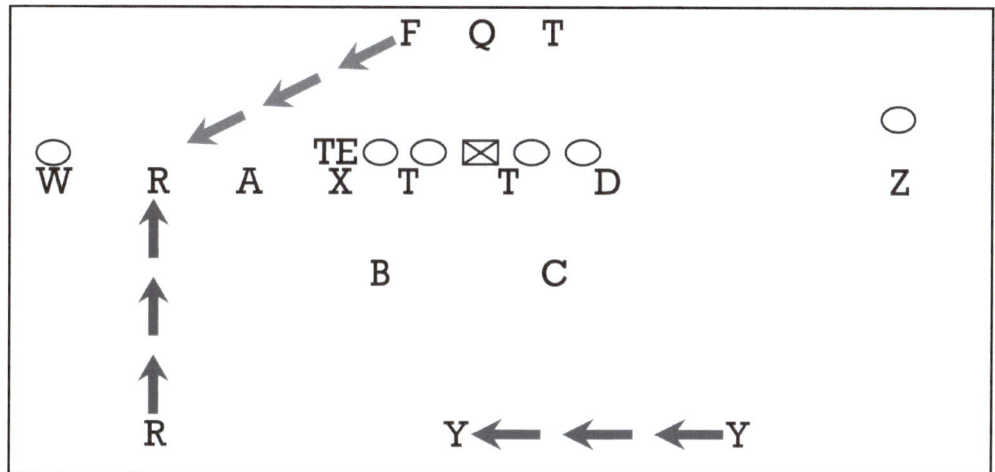

Diagram 61

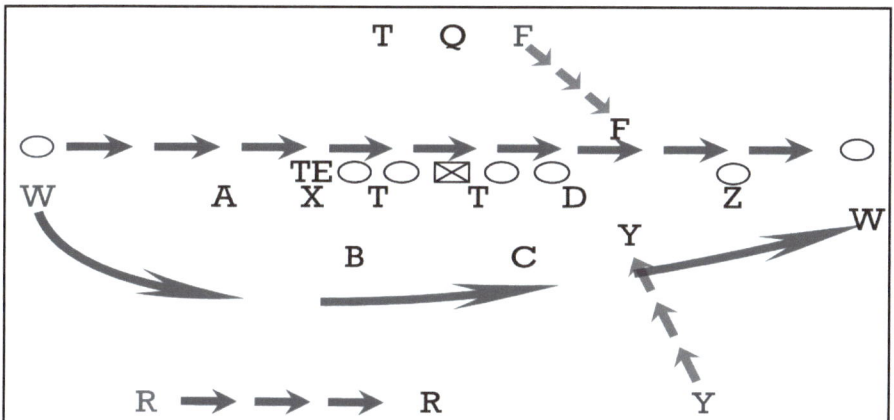

Diagram 62

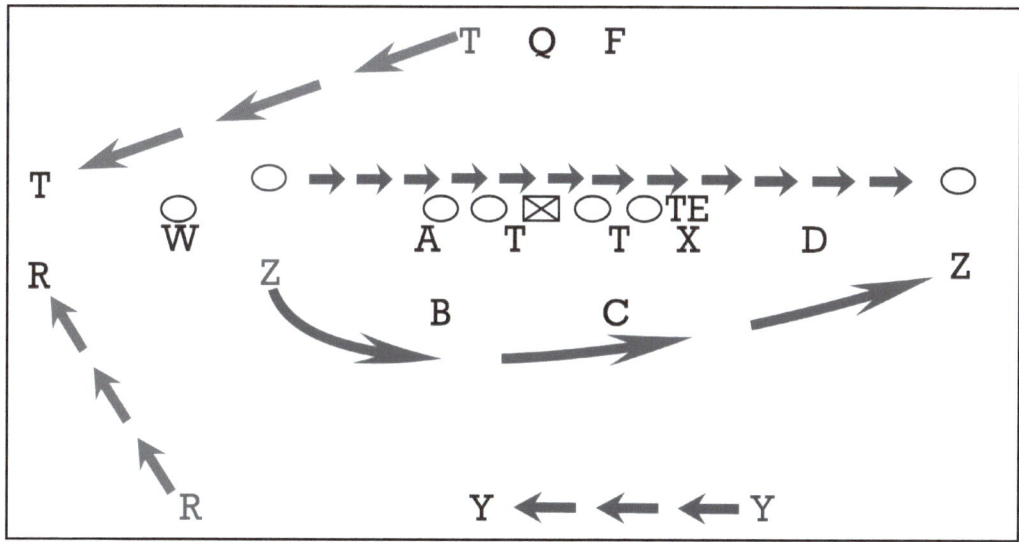

122 Diagram 63

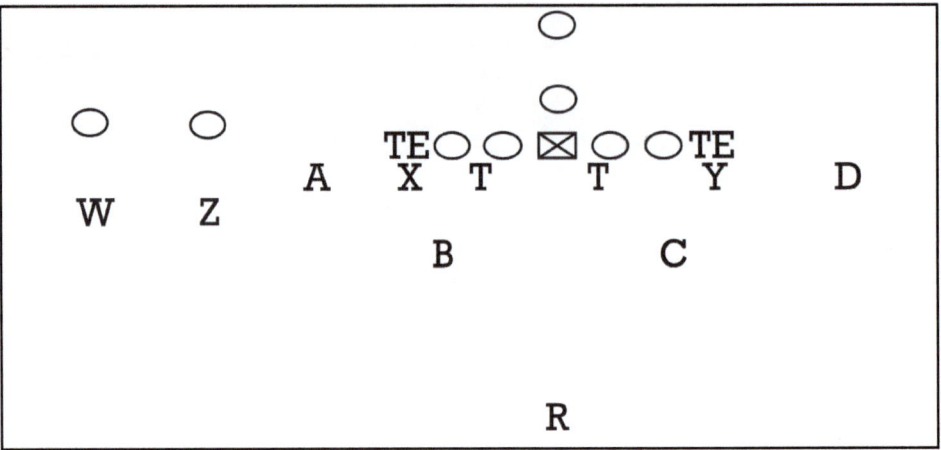

122 Diagram 64

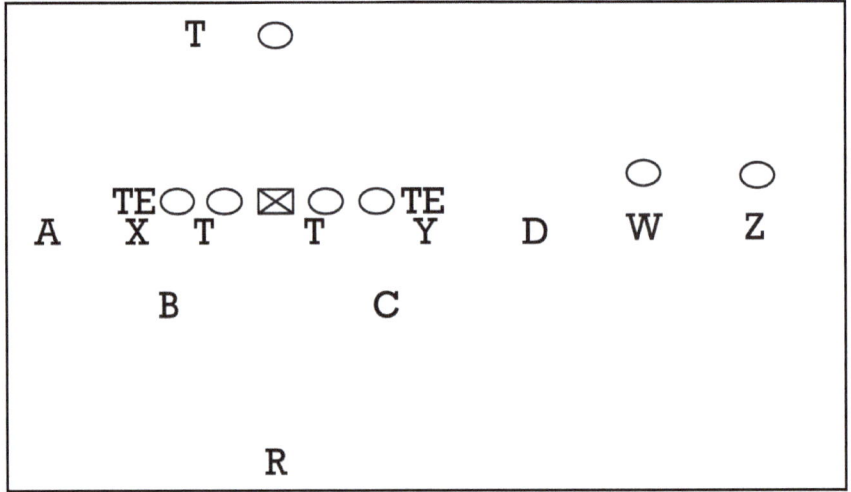

103 Left Diagram 65

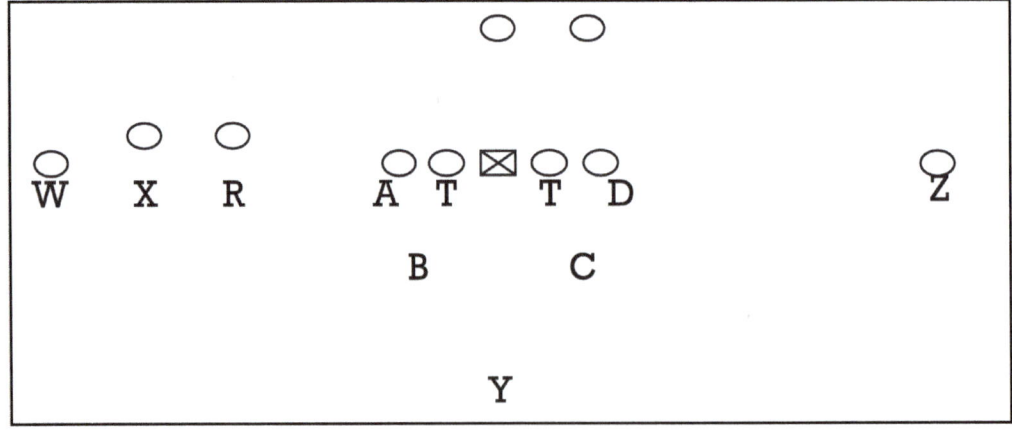

103 Right Diagram 66

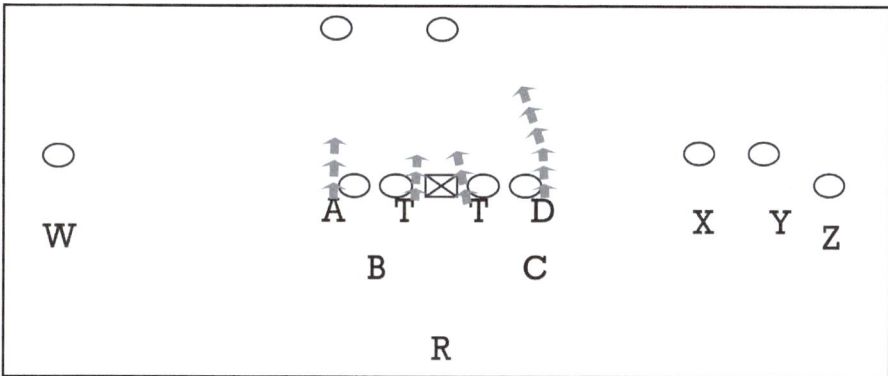

014 Diagram 67

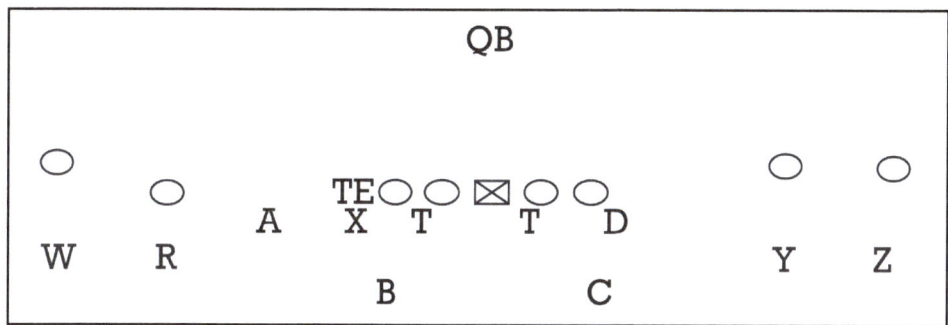

Diagram 68

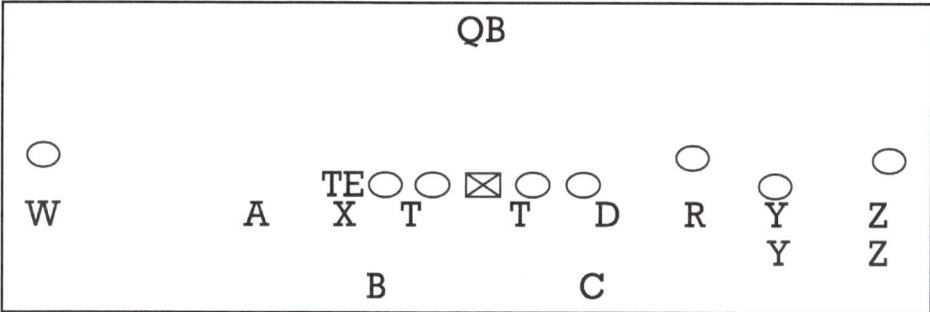

Diagram 69

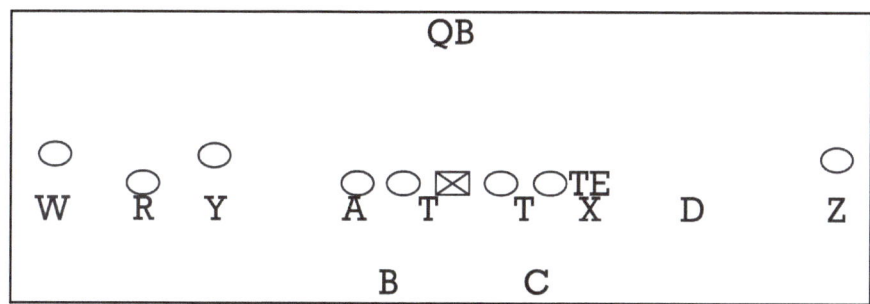

Diagram 70

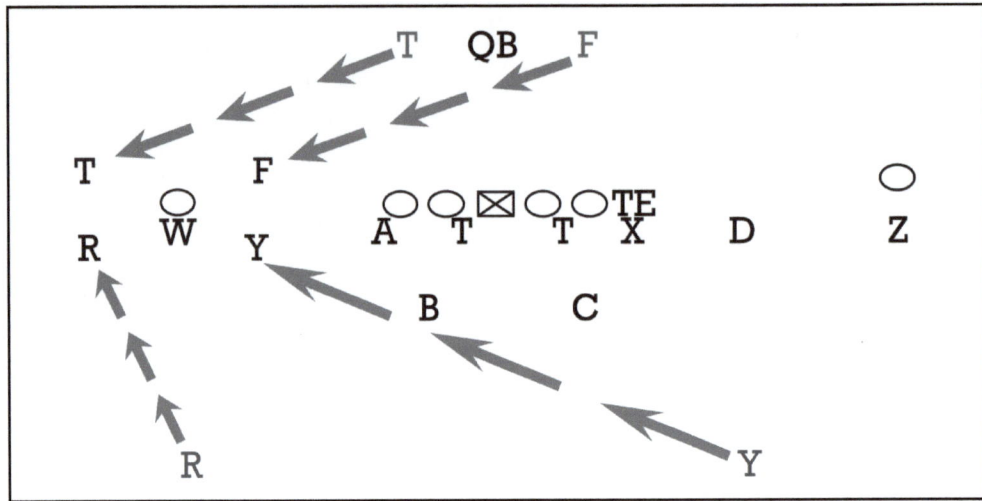

Diagram 71

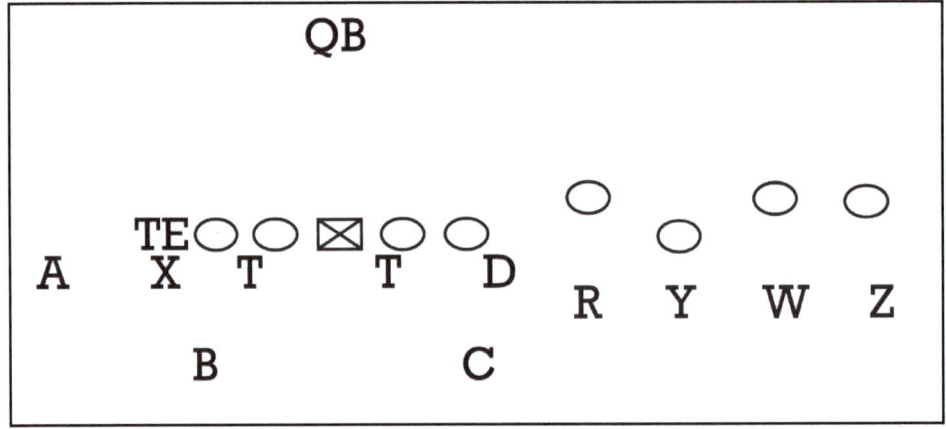

023 **Diagram 72**

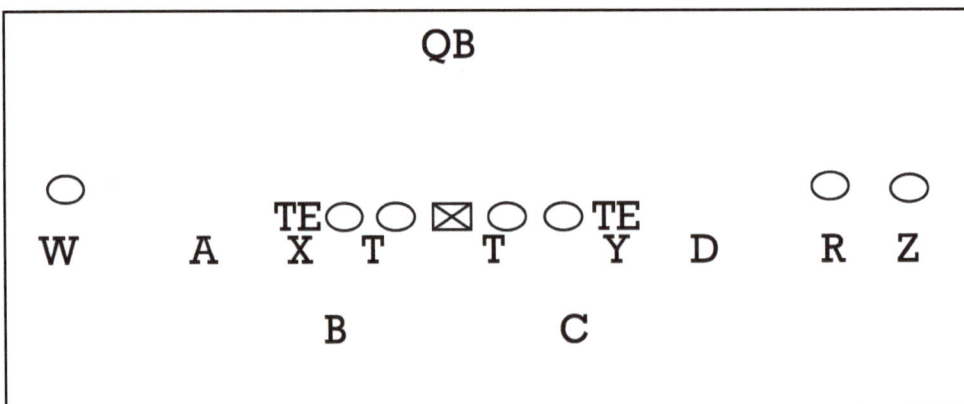

Diagram 73

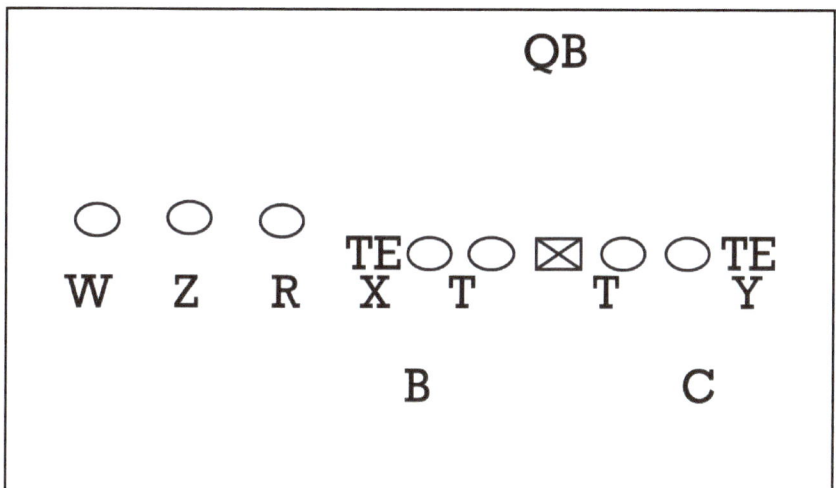

Diagram 74

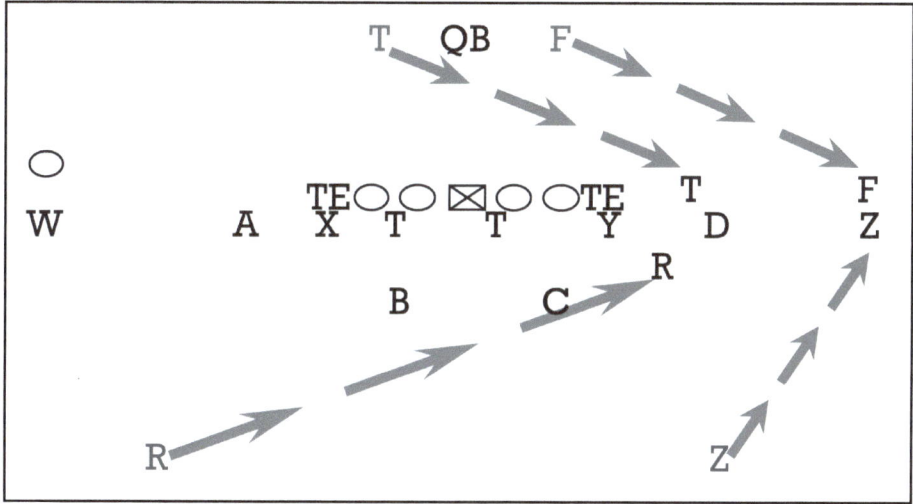

005 Diagram 75

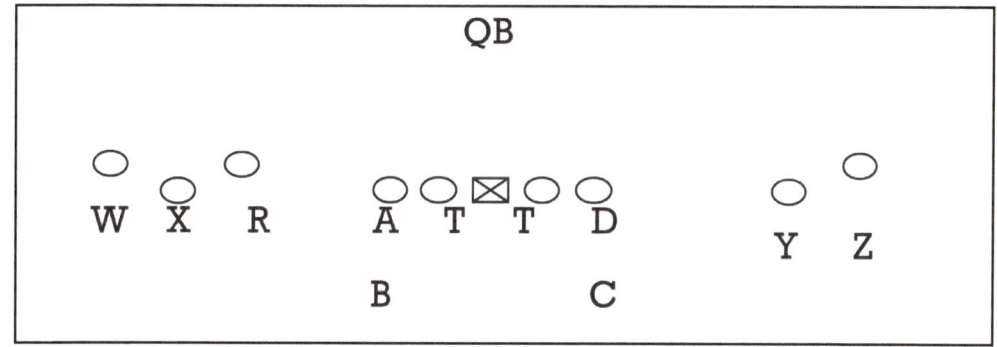

Diagram 76

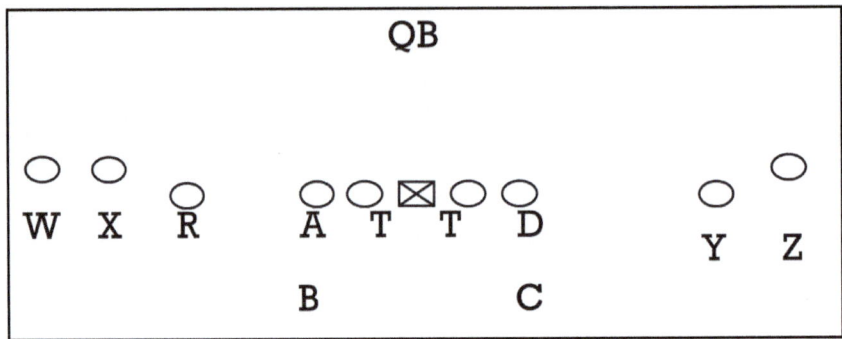

Diagram 77

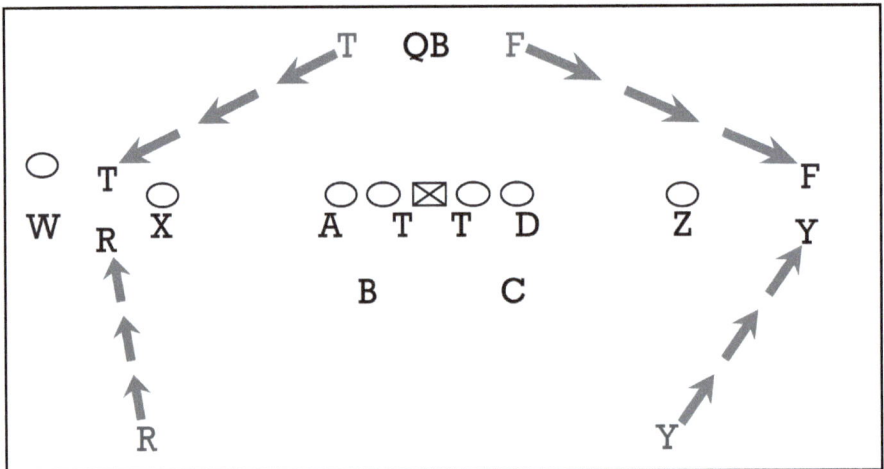

Summary:

- Coverage converts according to number of backs
- Deep shell matches number of backs
- 2 backs = cover 2
- 1 back = cover 1
- 0 backs = cover 0

Versus zero backs (empty), automatically apply max. pressure (6 rushers) versus 5 blockers to eliminate the Cover Zero risk. This is the only offensive formation that changes Charlie's assignment from low robber/spy to rusher and removes press coverage. We never rush only 5 with Cover Zero. Five rushers defeats the purpose of Cover Zero, which is to see who wins the race – the rush to the QB or the QBs release. The purpose of Cover Zero is to force a 3-step drop of a QB run but never allow a 5-7 step drop – ever. The purpose of removing the press is to allow the 5 DBs eyes into the backfield. Although the coverage is man, all eyes are on the QB for 2 reasons: (i) to attack a QB run, and (ii) attack a short pass. The best way we have found to intercept short passes on cover zero is by reading the QBs eyes first.

Chalkboard: Derivative Calls

The Stretch Play is only the starting point of the limitless SWAT Defensive system both pedagogically and strategically. After the Stretch Play is installed, the next step is to teach limitless capacity- how to make any call and how to make any call fit any situation. I use a 3–step teaching plan for SWAT101 that is taught concurrently, not consecutively:

Chalkboard – Phase 2 of limitless Diagrams, the next group of derivative plays that are introduced in SWAT101 following the STRETCH Play. The remaining Phases of derivative plays are in subsequent volumes of Deep Force.

i. Field dimensions: Theory of Pressure

What I teach is explained consecutively in this chapter but I don't teach it consecutively - I teach it concurrently for 2 reasons:

Contextual teaching is a remarkable instructional strategy. Contextual teaching uses a point-of-reference, ie: a specific play, and connects other learning outcome (ie: field dimensions and theory of pressure). It's impossible to fully understand the significance of field dimensions and theory of pressure by teaching it in isolation. Unattached learning outcomes are simply memorized, but not understood – the deeper meaning is lost. To go deep, build a context and connect learning outcomes;

Reality. In my reality, it's impossible to design a teaching blueprint that applies season after season. Uncertainty dominates our reality – not knowing who will stick it out, the time allotted for practice, where we will practice, and who we will be playing.

The 3-step teaching plan is based on my personal research during 40 seasons. It represents what is intended to be installed – a lesson bank. Phase 2 is not an exhaustive group of plays, nor is it etched in stone. What gets installed is based on need and availability.

i. Chalkboard Diagram 47 (3)

42 Mike -Code 12 - 912

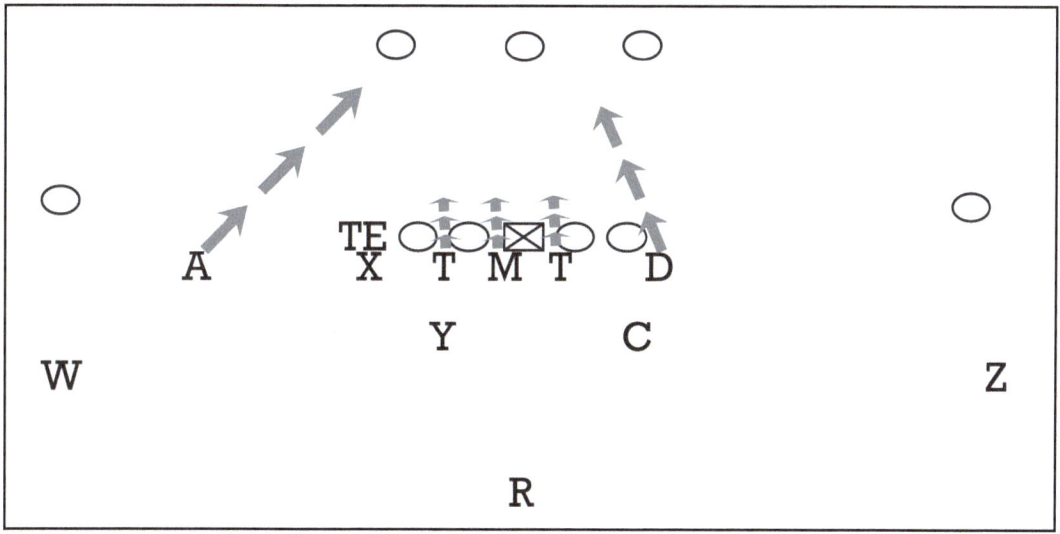

44 Mike - Code 12 - Charlie 2 - 912

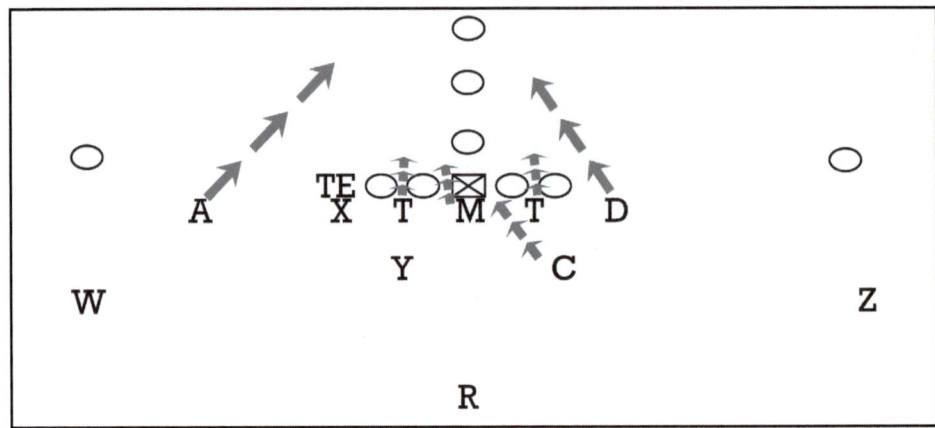

33 Bravo - Code 12 - 912

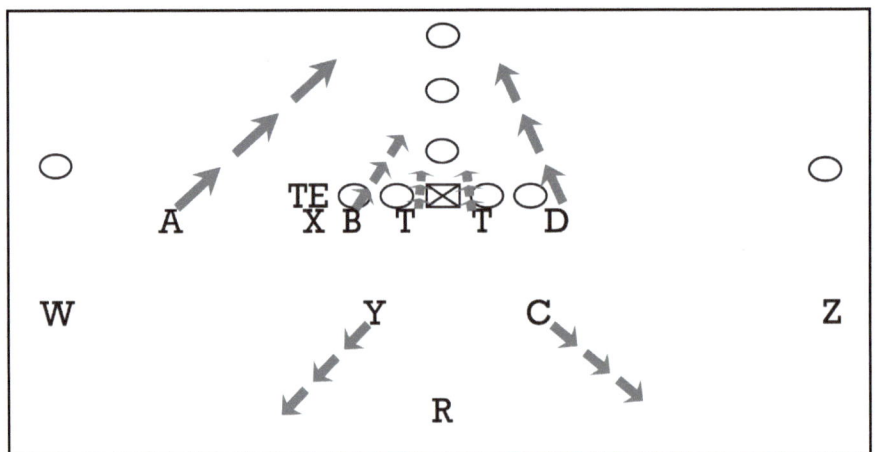

These Diagrams are an introductory sample of what can be designed and what I have used during the past 3 decades. The system is situation-specific. Every formation I have designed and used has had a purpose. Nothing has been randomly drawn up or used. All alignments and assignments solved a specific problem or fit a specific situation. Chalkboard illustrated derivatives of the Stretch Play, using only the 1st base Xpress concepts. Each play included only three variations of man coverage (2-deep man press, cover one man-free, and cover zero). Zone coverage will be the subject of subsequent issues of Deep Force.

ii. Field Dimensions

It is impossible to play defense without understanding field dimensions: (a) the distances separating field markings, and (b) zone sizes.

Defense depends of attacking at angles. Attacking the LOS, attacking the open field, and dropping to zones all require knowledge of distances that have to be traveled. The essentials of field dimensions are:

Distance between the ball and the sideline when the ball is spotted: (a) on a hash mark, or (b) at the mid-point between hash marks.

Width, depth and midpoints of zones.

I incorporate the significance of 10 distances in my teaching plan while installing the introductory phase of limitless formations :

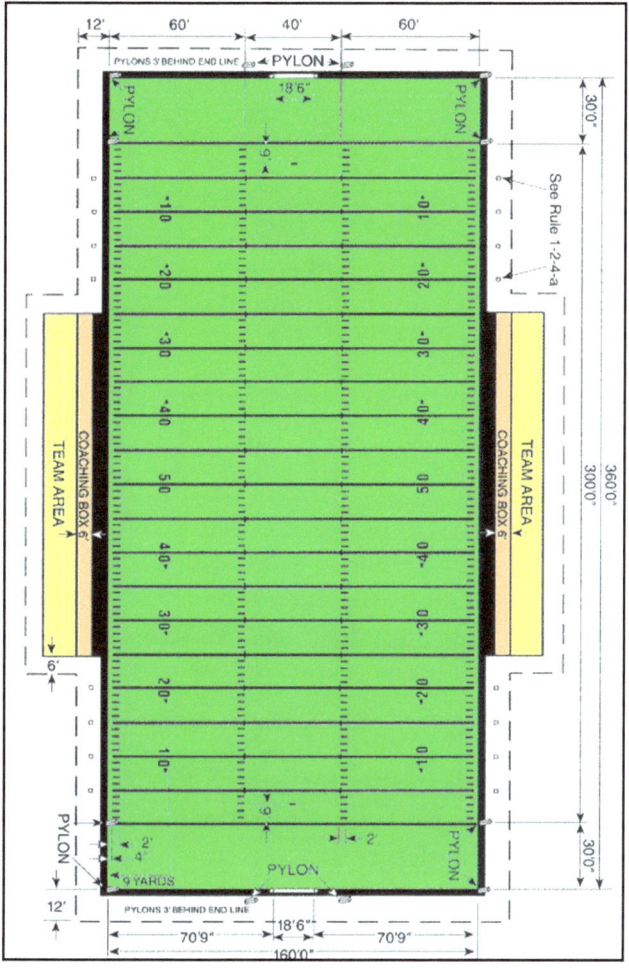

Key Points

The 10 distances are:

1. wide side from hash mark = 33.3 yards

2. short side from hash mark = 20 yards

3. distance between hash marks = 13.3 yards

4. balanced sides from midfield = 26.65 yards

5. distance between sideline and top of numbers = 9 yards

6. distance between top of sideline hash marks and sidelines = 2' 4"

7. 2 zones: width = 26.65 yards each. Mid-line seam for each zone = 13.325 yards. Close proximity landmarks are the mid-point between numbers and hash mark.

8. 3 zones: width = 17.7 yards. Mid-point seams = 8.8 yards. Close proximity landmark are the numbers + mid-field.

9. 4 zones width = 13.325 Mid-point seams = 6.7 yards. Close proximity landmarks are numbers + hash marks.

10. One zone – deep free = mid-field, mid-goalpost landmark with 2 equal sides of 26.65 yards

- One distance is not a constant – middle lane, referring to the horizontal seam separating deep and short zone. Our general rule is 15 yards from the LOS but that distance changes according to situation.

iii. Theory of Pressure

Pressure is the structured application of force, intentionally or unintentionally, real or perceived. Pressure is the central philosophy of the SWAT defense and the central Defensive Coordinator ideology in my DC Manual.

I wrote a defensive coordinator manual even though I've been my own DC for most of my head coach career. Several people have applied for the DC position. I use the manual as a decision-making model to decide whether to hire or not – a screening/selection process. And, the manual has been my vehicle for personal growth - a professional development research textbook.

I identified a number of specific competencies needed for DC selection. They are grouped into two general categories – content expertise and mind-set. DC mind-set starts with our Theory of Pressure, a –point model that governs out defensive thinking – teaching and decision-making.

Item 1 Pressure points

Pressure has to be structured. It needs direction and purpose. The design of structured pressure starts with, but is not limited to, the area behind the LOS. A concrete plan begins with pressure points, referring to the intended target or destination. The pressure point represents the aim point and establishes the road traveled

There are 5 pressure points that apply to both run and pass defense. They are grouped into 2 categories: (i) midline (ii) perimeter.

i) Midline: 3 pressure points – 3, 5 and 7

There are three midline pressure points that correspond with QB drops:

- "3" point is the 3-step drop (instruction: aim at 3 yards.)

- "5" point is the 5-step drop (instruction: aim at 5 yards)

- "7" point is the 7 step drop and the "escape route" (instruction: aim at 7 yards)

All 3 midline pressure points represent targets.

Diagram 81: Midline Pressure Points

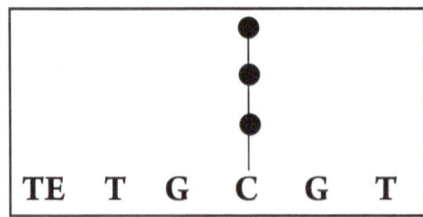

ii) Perimeter: 2 pressure points – 7RT and 7LT (7 yards behind the 2 OTs)

Perimeter pressure points are side entrances for FleXman rushers, who aim at 7 yards behind the tackles to reach their target.

Diagram 82: Perimeter Pressure Points

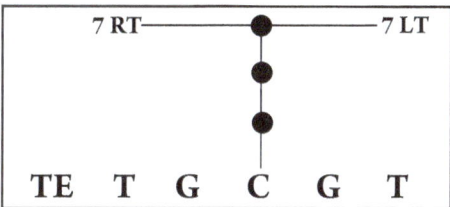

The 5 pressure points correspond to 8 LOS entrances. The combined effect of 8 LOS entrances and 5 pressure points correspond to the SWAT blitz system.

Item 2 BOB – Bind One Blocker

Blitzes are structured single-responsibility pressure paths. The unlimited blitz system is grouped into only 2 families or concepts of blitzes: (i) balanced (ii) overload.

The "balanced" concept features an equal number of single-responsibility rushers on both sides of the midline; "overload" has unbalanced numbers. The goal of both concepts is to bind at least one blocker – RB or OL.

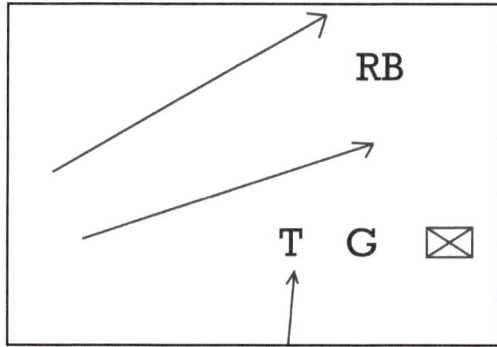

The concept of binding refers to forcing one blocker to decide which of two rushers to block. The bind is designed with two equally-spaced rushers adjacent to one blocker while all other blockers are occupied by being engaged in a block or have declared a block and cannot assist. Occupy and bind.

Item 3 FS/BS

Regardless whether it's pass or run, every play has a:

- ball-carrier
- ball-carier path
- frontside and a backside to the ballcarrier's path.

The FS/BS concept is basis of pursuit angles.

Item 4 RAT

Relentlessness, Angles, Tackling (RAT). These three elements will make any defensive system/concept successful – where to go, what to do upon arrival, and how to do both.

Item 5 ID TE

The DC is an uncertainty manager. He has to design methods of converting uncertainty to certainty through the combined effect of two types of research – pre-game research and game management research. Identifying the TE, the Big End, is the starting point. ID TE has 4 elements:
- presence or absence of a TE
- pre-snap activity (alignment and. re-alignment)
- post-snap movement (initial two steps and final path)
- what happens around the TE

Our research shows that the TE is usually the focal point of offensive strategy. Many offenses are strategically TE-oriented, referring to an intentional or unintentional trend of positioning the TE as the central focus of offensive strategy. "Focal point" is defined as the strategic center from which two things emerge: (i) habits/trends (ii) pre-snap indicators. The TE is defined as either the conventional TE position, the flex big or small end, or #2 receiver in a 4/5-receiver spread, regardless of that receiver's size.

The 4 elements of ID/TE provide three benefits:
- The most compelling profiling/scouting data.
- The best pre-snap defensive analysis.
- The key to defensive decision-making.
- After ID/TE is complete, the first step is coverage design centered around the TE – use the TE as the focal point of coverage strategy just as the OC uses the TE as the focal point of offensive strategy.

Item 6 2 P's – possession and points

Sustained maximum depends on objective-oriented mindset.

The word "defend" may be the biggest barrier to player development. The defense's purpose is not to defend – it is to get possession of the ball and score points. Defensive purpose is no different than offensive purpose – possession and points.

Item 7 Number of interior linemen plus one = number of gaps
- Single TE formations have 7 gaps (6+1).
- Double TE formation have 8 gaps (7+1).
- No TE formations have 6 gaps (5+1).
- IR (inside receiver/H-backs aligned 1x1 off the OT are the same as TE).
- The formula for number of gaps is: number of interior lineman plus one
- This formula is vital to determine whether a 6-rusher blitz is kept or canceled.
- This governs the first rule of blitz adjustment – count the gaps; one rusher per gap.

Item 8 Don't follow your teammate

This rule applies to all pursuit angles. A pass rush is a specific type of choreographed pursuit angles. Two pass rushers can never rush the same lane. Pass rushers must be equally spaced. Otherwise, the defense is playing with less than 11 men. Every rusher who rushes on a teammates track has reduced the number of defenders by one – the defense is playing with 10 players.

Two rushers on one track has to be avoided. Equally-spaced rushers is the adjustment rule when a bliter's departure point changes.

This governs the second rule of blitz adjustment – one rusher per track.

Item 9 Don't mix lessons

Never teach another coverage until the entire blitz system is taught within the base coverage. The reasons are: (i) the deeper meaning of blitzes is best understood when they are connected first to one coverage – the base coverage. The deeper meaning cannot be understood when coverages are taught one after another without teaching all the base blitzes that accompany the base coverage (ii) a thread of blitzes taught within the same coverage are additional cognitive reps that transfer the meaning of base coverage into long-term memory. The goal of staying in the base coverage is to reinforce how the coverage conversion decision-making model works. This is done by sticking to the base coverage and teaching all relevant blitzes before moving on to the second coverage. This method prevents recall errors and mental mistakes (iii) the next coverage is always an 'included' lesson – a derivative lesson. Coverage are not connected by themselves. Each coverage is a separate concept. Coverages are connected only by the entire blitz package associated to each coverage.

That's why mixing lessons doesn't work. Teaching a second coverage before all the base blitzes are taught is a mistake.

Item 10   Unbalanced blitzes overload one side

Two blitzes from the same side exponentially increases pressure. And when the side includes a flex rusher, the overload creates the most unique blocking bind possible – the bind created by C gap and flex lane rush. Blitzing the X-man(strong safety over the TE) represents the toughest blitz pickup for an offense because the X-man is inside the DE, creating blocking mismatches – if the blitzes are equally spaced.

Item 11   Disguise or not: the science of "showing blitz"

The defense can send messages to the offense by "showing a blitz" – tipping it off. The purpose is to create a predictable response – predictable blocking. When a SS blitzes from level 1, directly over the TE, moving the free safety above the blitzer is a give-away. The blitz is coming from the defender below the transferred DB.

Not showing a blitz has strengths also – no time for the offense to adjust to uncertainty. Changing-up these two strategies is too much for an offense to handle.

Item 12   45-degree track

In Cover 3 zone coverage, the 2 strong safeties align as FleXmen on Level 1. Their assignment is the 45 degree track. Versus run, sprint 45 degree to the side entrance of the #7 pressure point, representing the Stretch Play Track. Versus pass, sprint 45 degrees away from the LOS to the low part of the flat. If blitz is called, same track as versus run.

Item 13 No same level stunts/twists

In 1989, three level one stunts called in one game resulted in three explosive plays for the offense. Why? At the level I coach, our athletes do not have NFL or Division 1 speed. So, we abolished same-level stunts/twists. Why? Same level stunts and twist represent an exchange of rush lane/assignments by two defensive lineman. The exchange adds at least three steps by each DL to execute the exchange. My linemen do not have world class speed or quickness. A minimum of three extra steps adds time and distance to get to the lane and ballcarrier. And, mistakes are deadly. If the wrong angle is taken or wrong footwork is used, blockers will look like All-World blockers.

My defensive lineman are in the developmental process, trying to master the art of rushing straight upfield against accomplished blockers. Countless reps are need to master that skill. By the time that skill is mastered, they graduate. Exchanging rush lanes through stunts/twists takes away reps from the real skill of learning to rush straight upfield. A one-man coaching staff cannot teach both skills and there aren't enough reps in a season to master both skills.

Item 14 Limit the number of dual-responsibility players

Reduce the number of dual-responsibility players. Increase the number of single-responsibility players. Two reasons why:

   i. It is much easier to perform one job instead of two.

   ii. It is much easier to move forward than backward.

Item 15 Overload often and early

Unbalanced blitzes are 4 times stronger than balanced blitzes. Sending more rushers from one side of the midline is far more potent than sending equal number of rushers – especially during the first 2 drives of every game, regardless of opponent. The following is our teaching plan:

41-Code 14, XB 51, 921 <mark>Diagram 83</mark>

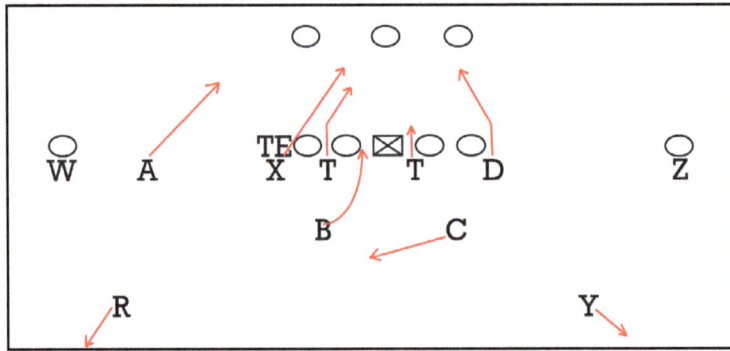

Key points

- X-ray blitzes left/strongside C gap (5 hole).

- Bravo blitzes left/strongside A gap (1 hole).

- XB 51 means X blitzes 5, B blitzes 1.

- The AX rush forms an equally-spaced 75-degree and 45-degree rush that creates the most challenging blocking bind because of width of the flex rusher.

- 921 instructs the 2 deep safeties to drop to deep-halves (stay in Cover 2). The TE will be picked up by one of the 3 zone defenders if the TE's route near the middle or deep. The weakness is the flat pass - if TE sprints to the flat, he should be open. Theoretically, it looks like giving up the flat pass to the TE. We're not. The best way to defend a flat pass is pressure the QB. The next Diagram shows the alternative coverage.

41-Code 14, XB 51, 911 Diagram 84

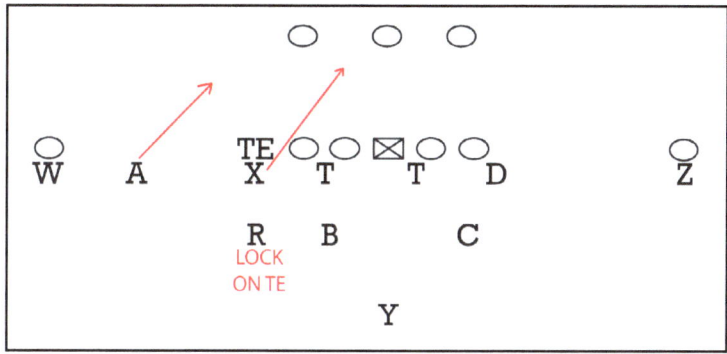

Key Points

- 911 means cover 1. This instructs Robber and Yankee to convert to Cover 1. As the QB gets set, Robber moves into the box, directly over the TE. R assumes X's assignment.

- Y realigns onto the midline.

- The strength is the 8-man box and the inability to block R on a running play.

- The weakness is a crossfield route by the TE. If the TE releases at 30 degrees inside, R will be at a disadvantage.

- Both calls can be used with the corners offline (922 or 912) and against 21 shotgun. 2-back shotgun does not require an adjustment.

41-Code 14, XB 51, 912 Diagram 85

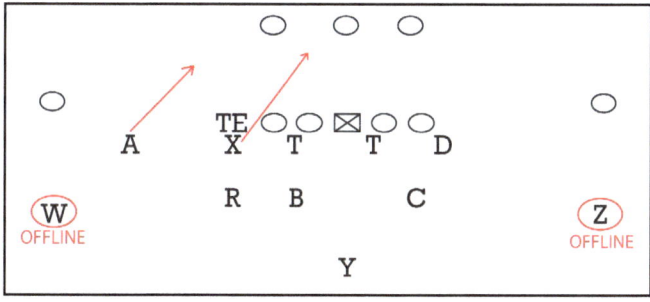

Key Point:

- 912 means: 9= "coverage is", 1=cover 1, 2= corners offline.

83

41- Code 12 XB 51 – 912 Diagram 86

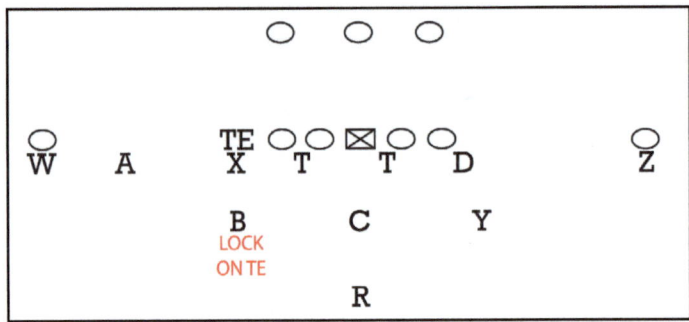

Key Points
- This call introduces CODE 12 – X on Level 1, Y on Level 2.
- The offensive formation has 7 gaps.
- When Y has level 2 responsibility, he becomes the 3rd LB, forming 3 equally-spaced LB.
- Bravo moves to MLB and keeps the code-name Bravo, not Mike.
- Which side Y aligns on depends on whether X blitzes: (a) if X blitzes, Y aligns directly behind X on level 2. Two strong safeties on the same side – stacked strong safeties; (b) if X does not blitz, Y aligns on the right side over the inside receiver (IR) spot, whether or not an IR is aligned there. In that case, the LO order will be Bravo, Charlie (MLB), Yankee.
- Delta aligns nose-on the OT and defends B gap.
- The XB 51 blitz stays – no audible, Bravo blitzes from the MLB spot.
- This unconventional alignment cannot be blocked fully.

Converting XB 51 blitz from Code 14
- Can the blitz happen? Is it mathematically possible?
- If the blitz can mathematically happen, keep it. If it can't, cancel it.
- These questions govern whether the call remains or if it changes.
- XB 51 with 922 coverage means 6 rush and 5 cover. The 5 coverage are divided as 2 man and 3 zone. The goal is to keep the blitz against as many formations as possible.
- Versus 4 receivers, apply the decision-making model as follows:

1. **Versus 11 2x2 = 7 gaps with 4 receivers. Convert to 902 (cover zero with CBs offline) and keep the blitz Diagram 87**

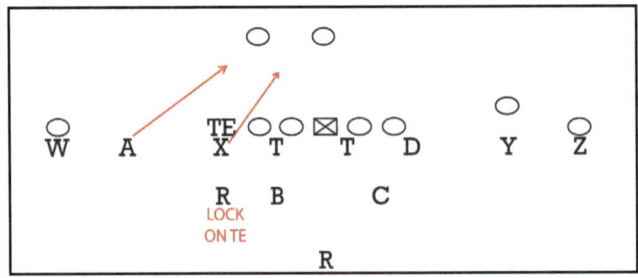

2. **Versus 11 1x3= same, 7 gaps with 4 receivers. Convert to 902 and keep the blitz Diagram 88**

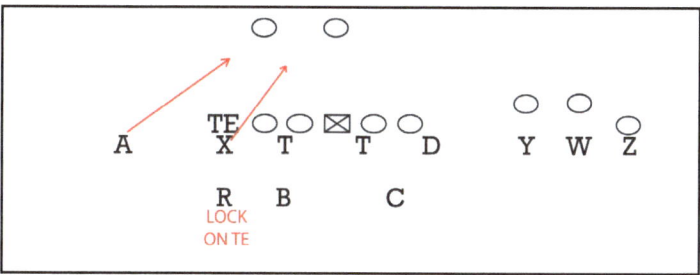

3. **Versus 10 2x2 Diagram 89**

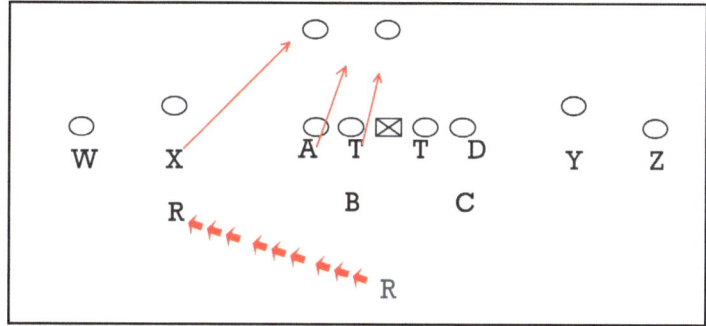

Key Points

- 6 gaps with 4 receivers. One less gap. In accordance with the model, X aligns over #2 while Alpha (DE) moves over the DE. Mathematically, the XB 51 blitz can be kept with the following changes governed by the 2 rules of blitz adjustment:

(i) count the gaps – one rusher per gap

(ii) don't follow your teammate – equally spaced rushers. One rusher per track.

- The following changes are needed:

    - Convert to 902 (cover zero, CBs offline).

    - X aligns directly over #2, no shade.

    - Robber aligns 8 yards over #2, showing the blitz.

    - Alpha aligns nose-on the OT, directly over the OT without a shade.

    - Blitz path are:

        i. X from flex at 75 degrees

        ii. Alpha at 45 degrees into C gap

        iii. LDT 30 degree in

4. Versus 01 3x2 Diagram 90

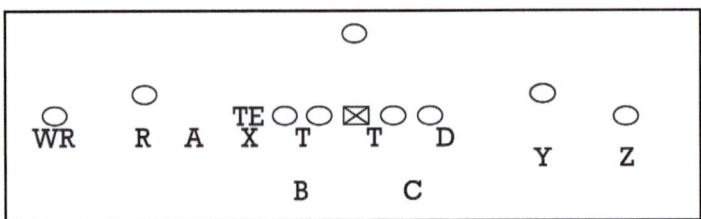

Robber cannot compensate for the X blitz and the model calls for both ILBs (Bravo and Charlie to blitz) versus an empty backfield. Mathematically, the XB 51 blitz doesn't fit.

Convert to cover zero, 5 DBs cover man on the 5 receivers and 6 in the box blitz. Same effect, different call

5. Versus 01 2x3 = same as previous – convert to zero, follow the model. Diagram 91

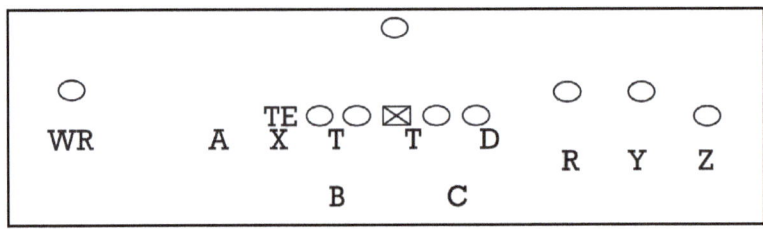

Emergency call = 10-78 (police language for 'needs assistance').

Translation – cancel the entire call.

Convert to man + CBs offline + follow the model

41 Code 12, XB 51, 902 Diagram 92

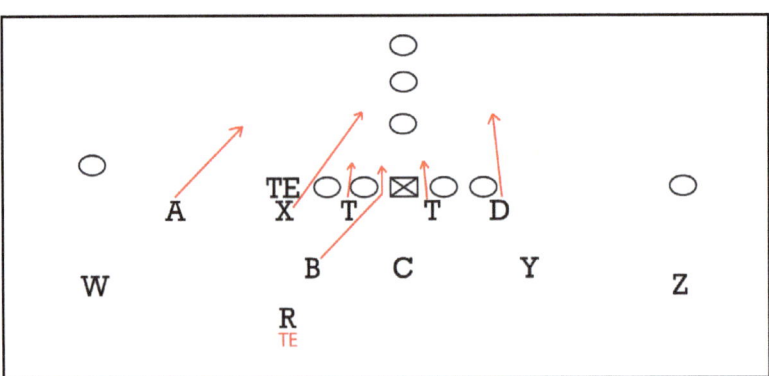

Key Points
- Y re-aligns to level 2 as LB.
- R Cover TE, converting man/free Cover 1 to 902 Cover Zero.

42 Mike Code 12 Diagram 93

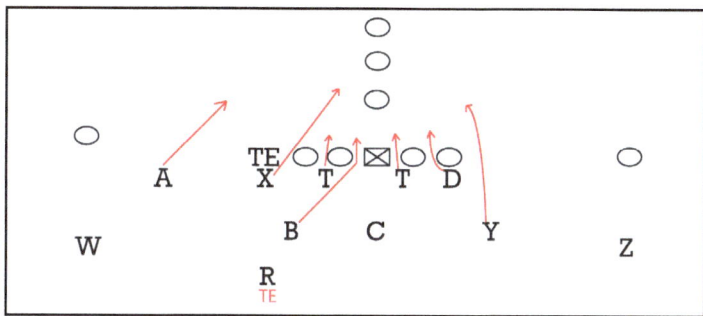

42 Mike Code 12, 921 Diagram 94

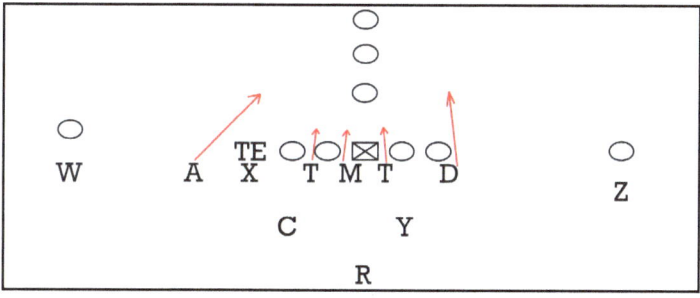

Key Points
- "MIKE" realigns Bravo to Level 1 into Strong A. He automatically rushes. Same assignments, different alignment.
- Y aligns as LB at level 2.
- C and Y align equally spaced - B Gaps.

Failure is a wake-up call that either moves you toward your dream - or ends it. The response to failure is what matters. Either get up and fix what's broken or blame every one and everything, and quit. The gift of free will.

– Soul of a Lifter

END OF VOLUME ONE...
to be continued

Bibliography
References and Footnotes

All things must pass – including conventional thinking.

When I started my Master's degree and later, my PhD dissertation, I was steered toward a large volume of literature that, at the time, seemed irrelevant to coaching football and strength coaching, two professions that I had researched over many years, through repeated case study analysis – case studies involving athletes I had coached. But, page after page, my attitude changed – about everything.

The list below, of remarkable literature, has deeply influenced my philosophy about football coaching, strength coaching, college law enforcement teaching, business, and leadership. Not only did it form the core of my Master's degree and partial PhD dissertation, the combined effect of this list confirmed some of my beliefs while shaping others, including:

- Think outside the box – the deeper the better.

- Keep track of what you do – like in policing, keep copious notes – record everything.

- Figure out what works in your reality and keep doing it – believe in what you do.

Work your ass off. Hard work trumps DNA. Genetics influence what we become but talent and expertise are developed – it doesn't just happen. Nothing just happens.

To facilitate the footnote process, I have grouped the list of literature by titles, summarizing their conclusions. Numbered footnotes, throughout the volume of text, correspond to the reference within the text. Other authors are credited for their contribution to the text, in the following summation.

∞

Developing Expertise

Experts are not born, they are made. Peak performers are developed, not born.

- The 10-year rule.

- The 10,000 hour rule.

Ericsson, K Anders, Charness, N., Feltovich, P., and Hoffman, R. R. (Eds.) (2006). Cambridge handbook of expertise and expert performance. Cambridge, UK: Cambridge University Press.

Ericsson, K. Anders, Krampe, Ralf Th., and Tesch-Romer, Clemens. (1993) The role of deliberate practice in the acquisition of expert performance. Psychological Review 1993, Vol. 100, No. 3, 363-406 Copyright 1993 by the American Psychological Association, Inc. 0033-295X/93/S3.00.

Bloom, Benjamin. S., and Sosniak, L.A. (1985). Developing talent in young people. New York: Ballantine Books.

Leonard, Dorothy, and Swap, Walter C. (2005) Deep smarts. Harvard Business Press.

∞
Motivation:
Cognitive dissonance, flow, meaning

Cognitive Dissonance: the inner tension caused by not acting in accordance with our beliefs.

Festinger, Leon. (1957). A theory of cognitive dissonance. Evanston, IL: Row, Peterson.
Flow: the struggle between anxiety and boredom determines the level of performance.

Csikszentmihalyi, Mihaly. (1990). Flow: The psychology of optimal experience. New York: Harper and Row.

There is a relationship between meaning and performance – what matters is a powerful motivator.

Frankl, Viktor. (1959) Man's search for meaning. Beacon Press: Boston, Mass.

∞

Personality:
Characteristics of a peak performer

Reming, George. (1987) Personality characteristics of supercops and habitual criminals. A dissertation presented to the faculty of the California Graduate Institute. Los Angeles, California.

Rogers, Carl. (1961). On becoming a person: a therapist's view of psychotherapy. London: Constable. ISBN 1-84529-057-7.

∞

Experts see the whole board,
not the individual pieces.

de Groot, A.D. (1978). Thought and choice in chess (rev. translation, 1946; 2nd ed.). The Hague, the Netherlands: Mouton.

Gobet, F. and Simon, H.A. (1996). Templates in chess memory: a mechanism for recalling several boards. Cognitive Psychology, 31. 1-40.

Leonard, Dorothy and Swap, Walter C. (2005) Deep smarts. Harvard Business Press.

∞

Reaching full potential: 2 blockers.

The Colgan Institute identified two major obstacles to development of full potential:

- cosseting, defined as indulging students by permitting inappropriate, immature behaviour that weakens and creates dependency, and

- insufficient challenge – failure to raise the bar and inject learning rigor compatible with the level of instruction prevents personal growth and motivation. Protecting students from failure is an obstacle to reaching full potential.

∞

The 66% Conformity Rule

The majority of people will adopt the observations and beliefs of others even if it contradicts their own beliefs.

Milgram, Stanley (1963). "Behavioral Study of Obedience". Journal of Abnormal and Social Psychology 67: 371–378. doi:10.1037/h0040525. PMID 14049516. http://content.apa.org/journals/abn/67/4/371. Full-text PDF.

Milgram, Stanley. (1974). Obedience to authority; an experimental view. Harpercollins (ISBN 0-06-131983-X).

Asch, S. E. (1951). Effects of group pressure upon the modification and distortion of judgment. In H. Guetzkow (ed.) Groups, leadership and men. Pittsburgh, PA: Carnegie Press.

Guerilla Ontology: extremes can be transformational, building positive change

Wilson, Robert Anton (1975). The illuminatus trilogy. New Falcon Publications.

Enjoy the book?
We would like to hear from you.

Post a review on Amazon, Goodreads or let us know directly at reviews@ginoarcaro.com.

Follow Gino & Jordan Publications Inc. on Social Media

- GinoArcaro *or* GinoArcarco.Author
- @Gino_Arcaro *or* @JordanPubInc.
- +GinoArcaro *or* +GinoArcaroBooks
- GinoArcaro
- Gino's Blog

More Books by Gino Arcaro

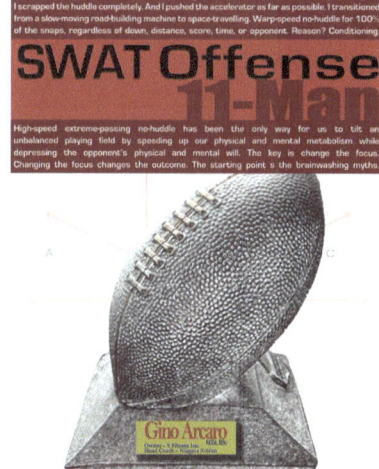

SWAT Offense
By connecting partial concepts that can build any formation, any pass play and any running play to fit the situation, at the line of scrimmage, Arcaro has designed a system that eliminates the need for a conventional playbook that has to be memorized. Memorization is replaced by translation of a simple language. He designed the SWAT offense as a solution to a nightmarish reality of limitations – poor talent and poor resources, a one-man coaching staff, open-admission players, and on top of it all, out-matched opponents willingly sought out! David constantly calling out Goliath. Arcaro's SWAT offense is the most unique offensive system you'll ever see because it has limitless offense capacity but no playbook. A unique feature of the SWAT Offense is its ties to SWAT Defense.

4th & Hell Season 1
"We were David with a Canadian passport, failing miserably at winning just one football game against stars-and-stripes-draped Goliaths." It came down to fourth and hell – a face-to-face showdown. No disguises, no masks, no secret weapons. No one huddled on the sideline. No one huddled on the field. Both sides knew what to expect. No surprises, no guess-work, no mind games. Making the call was a formality. All that mattered was running the play to see what would pass. Someone would execute; someone would be executed.

eXplode: X Fitness Training System

Sought after his entire adult life to help others achieve their workout goals, Arcaro put his weight lifting theories and routines into this manual. His "Case Studies," true stories from his 40+ years of working out (completely natural) bring a sense of reality to the average gym-goer who just wants to get in shape, stay in shape, and most-importantly, not quit. No gimmicks, just discussion and formulas that can be tailored to any situation regardless of how long or how intensely one has been working out.

Soul of a Lifter

Gino Arcaro's journey from childhood obesity to natural health and strength was not made alone; he relied on the Soul of a Lifter. In telling this tale, Arcaro draws on life lessons learned from his careers as a football coach, police officer and college teacher to inspire and lead the reader in a soul-searching quest to reach his/her own potential. This is not your run-of-the-mill motivational book. Discover insights about what drives the soul… what happens when you listen and when you don't!

Selling H.E.L.L. in Hell
from the series Soul of an Entrepreneur

You may be starting out in business or just contemplating making the big decision. Gino Arcaro knows what you're thinking and wants to make sure you know what you're not thinking. His thought-bending tales, while entertaining and steeped in reality, will make the would-be business owner take a second and third look at the situation before jumping in. And, for those already "self-employed," Arcaro offers a unique slant on dealing with day-to-day customer and employee challenges.

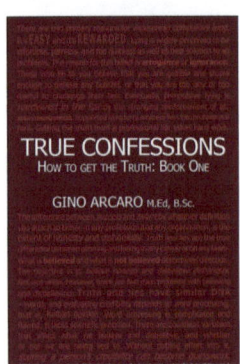

True Confessions

Gino Arcaro relates and upholds a simple fact: "Everyone has a conscience. No exceptions. If you're alive, you have a conscience. The myth of 'no conscience' actually means 'weak or dysfunctional' conscience." Therefore, a truth-seeker must appeal to the conscience, meaning, "make the conscience work out, make it work right, and make it do all the work." True Confessions is a manual for anyone whose job it is to get the truth. For example, Human Resources personnel during the job interview process or Law Enforcement interviewers who can use Arcaro's theories to open a window into the psyche of a suspect under interrogation.

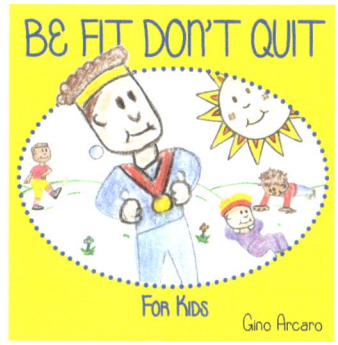
BE FIT DON'T QUIT
Full of exercise ideas young children can try on their own or with a parent, this book will rekindle in any adult a love for the simple act of playing. Gino Arcaro has spent his life working out and teaching young adults about the importance of "being fit." He wrote Be Fit Don't Quit to express a tried-and-true message: Exercising is natural and fun. Never quit!

BEAUTY OF A DREAM
Inspired by the birth of his first grandchild, Arcaro wrote this colour picture-infused booklet to encourage the reader to dream, dream big and never stop dreaming. "No one can break into your dream and rob you of it, unless you let them." His message, in this book as in all his works, is a challenge for the reader to strive to reach his/her potential and make an impact in this world. A perfect gift for someone in your life who needs to be "lifted" or reminded that dreaming is important!

For more free book previews or to purchase Gino's books go to
WWW.GINOARCARO.COM

www.ingramcontent.com/pod-product-compliance
Lightning Source LLC
Chambersburg PA
CBHW040059160426
43193CB00002B/23